Quantum Dreams

Samuel Park's Subatomic Discoveries

Morgan Williams

ISBN: 9781779666048
Imprint: Press for Play Books
Copyright © 2024 Morgan Williams.
All Rights Reserved.

Contents

Introduction   1
The Mysterious Life of Samuel Park   1

The Spark of Inspiration   13
A Chance Encounter with a Brilliant Scientist   13

Bibliography   23

The Unconventional Path   25
Breaking Free from Traditional Scientific Methods   25

The Subatomic World Unveiled   35
Samuel's First Major Breakthrough: The Quantum Microscope   35

The Race for the Nobel Prize   45
Recognition and Validation of Samuel's Contributions   45

Unraveling the Secrets of the Universe   57
Quantum Entanglement: Samuel's Greatest Discovery   57

Samuel's Legacy   67
Inspiring the Next Generation of Innovators   67

Bibliography   77

Conclusion   79
Samuel Park: Pioneer of Subatomic Discoveries   79

Index   89

Introduction

The Mysterious Life of Samuel Park

Early Childhood and Curiosity

Samuel Park was born in a small town, nestled between rolling hills and vibrant fields, in a family that valued knowledge and exploration. From an early age, Samuel exhibited a curious mind, constantly asking questions about the world around him. His parents, both educators, nurtured his inquisitiveness, encouraging him to explore the natural world. This environment fostered a sense of wonder that would later propel him into the depths of quantum mechanics.

Samuel's childhood was marked by a series of exploratory adventures. He would often be found in his backyard, dissecting insects or collecting rocks, each specimen sparking questions that seemed to have no end. This insatiable curiosity was not just a passing phase; it was the foundation of his future scientific endeavors. His early explorations can be likened to the scientific method itself, where observation leads to hypothesis, experimentation, and ultimately, discovery.

The Influence of Family

The Park household was a treasure trove of knowledge. Samuel's mother, a biology teacher, often brought home science kits and books filled with illustrations of the microscopic world. His father, a physics professor, would engage Samuel in discussions about the universe, often using humor to make complex topics more relatable. For instance, he would joke, "Why did the photon refuse to check a bag at the airport? Because it was traveling light!" Such light-hearted exchanges made learning enjoyable and accessible, instilling in Samuel the belief that science was not just a discipline but a way of viewing the world.

One pivotal moment in Samuel's early life occurred when he was just seven years old. During a family trip to a science museum, he encountered a demonstration on the principles of light and optics. The vibrant colors produced by prisms captivated him, leading him to wonder about the nature of light itself. This fascination would later evolve into a deep interest in quantum mechanics, where the behavior of light at a subatomic level would become a central theme in his research.

Education and Early Scientific Interests

As Samuel progressed through elementary school, his curiosity only deepened. He thrived in science classes, often outpacing his peers in understanding complex concepts. His teachers noted his ability to connect ideas across different scientific disciplines, a skill that would serve him well in his future studies. For example, during a project on ecosystems, Samuel drew parallels between the interdependence of species and the interconnectedness of particles in physics, showcasing his ability to think critically and creatively.

Despite his academic prowess, Samuel faced challenges typical of gifted children. He often felt isolated from his peers, who struggled to understand his intense interests. This sense of alienation was compounded by a few teachers who dismissed his ideas as fanciful or overly ambitious. However, Samuel's family remained his steadfast supporters, encouraging him to pursue his passions regardless of external skepticism.

Challenges and Setbacks

In middle school, Samuel encountered a significant setback when he attempted to present a project on quantum mechanics at the school science fair. His ambitious proposal was met with skepticism from both judges and classmates. "Why would you want to study something so small that you can't even see it?" one judge remarked. This experience was disheartening; however, it also served as a turning point. Samuel realized that the path of innovation is often fraught with challenges and that perseverance is key.

Motivated by this experience, Samuel began to embrace his uniqueness. He found solace in books about famous scientists who faced similar adversities. Reading about figures like Albert Einstein, who was once considered a poor student, inspired him to push through the doubts cast by others. He adopted a mantra: "Curiosity is the fuel for discovery," reminding himself that every question asked was a step toward understanding.

The Dream of Discovering the Subatomic World

By the time he reached high school, Samuel's passion for science had crystallized into a dream: to uncover the mysteries of the subatomic world. He spent countless hours in the school library, poring over texts that described the bizarre behavior of particles and the principles of quantum mechanics. His fascination with the topic was not merely academic; it was a profound yearning to understand the fundamental building blocks of reality.

In his junior year, Samuel participated in a summer program at a local university, where he was introduced to advanced topics in physics. It was here that he first encountered the concept of quantum entanglement, a phenomenon that would later become central to his research. The idea that particles could be interconnected across vast distances, instantaneously affecting one another, captivated him. Samuel often likened this concept to a cosmic joke, where the universe seemed to playfully defy the conventional laws of physics.

This early dream of exploring the subatomic world was not without its challenges. Samuel grappled with the abstract nature of quantum mechanics, often finding himself lost in equations and theories that seemed to contradict common sense. However, he approached these challenges with the same curiosity that had defined his childhood. He began to see complex equations, such as the Schrödinger equation:

$$i\hbar\frac{\partial}{\partial t}\Psi(\mathbf{r},t) = \hat{H}\Psi(\mathbf{r},t) \tag{1}$$

as puzzles to be solved rather than insurmountable obstacles. This shift in perspective was crucial, allowing him to embrace the complexities of quantum physics with enthusiasm rather than fear.

In conclusion, Samuel Park's early childhood was characterized by an insatiable curiosity, a supportive family environment, and a series of challenges that would shape his future endeavors. His journey from a curious child to a budding scientist was marked by a relentless pursuit of knowledge and a dream to explore the subatomic world. This foundational period not only ignited his passion for science but also instilled in him the resilience needed to navigate the complexities of the scientific landscape. Samuel's story serves as a reminder that curiosity, when nurtured, can lead to groundbreaking discoveries and innovations.

Family Influence and Encouragement

Samuel Park's journey into the world of science was significantly shaped by the environment in which he was raised. His family, a vibrant tapestry of diverse backgrounds and professions, played a crucial role in nurturing his innate curiosity and passion for discovery. This section explores the influence of Samuel's family and the encouragement he received that ultimately propelled him toward his groundbreaking work in quantum mechanics.

From an early age, Samuel was surrounded by discussions that sparked his imagination. His mother, an elementary school teacher, often brought home stories of scientific wonders, from the mysteries of the solar system to the intricacies of plant biology. Samuel would listen with wide eyes as she described how plants convert sunlight into energy through photosynthesis, a process that would later resonate with his understanding of energy at the quantum level. The equation governing this process can be simplified to:

$$\text{Photosynthesis: } 6CO_2 + 6H_2O \xrightarrow{light} C_6H_{12}O_6 + 6O_2 \qquad (2)$$

This equation not only illustrates a fundamental biological process but also embodies the beauty of scientific inquiry that Samuel would come to appreciate.

His father, a physicist with a penchant for experimental science, often engaged Samuel in discussions about the nature of reality. They would spend evenings tinkering with simple circuits and conducting home experiments, such as building a rudimentary electromagnet. These hands-on experiences instilled in Samuel the importance of experimentation and the scientific method. His father would often quote Richard Feynman, saying, "The first principle is that you must not fool yourself—and you are the easiest person to fool." This mantra became a guiding principle for Samuel as he navigated the complexities of scientific research.

However, Samuel's path was not without its challenges. As a child, he faced moments of self-doubt, especially when he struggled with mathematics. His family recognized these challenges and provided unwavering support. His mother would sit with him for hours, patiently guiding him through complex equations and encouraging him to see mathematics as a language of the universe rather than a barrier. This nurturing approach not only improved his mathematical skills but also fostered a sense of resilience. Samuel learned that setbacks were merely stepping stones to greater understanding.

The encouragement extended beyond academics. Samuel's family celebrated his small victories, whether it was a successful science project or a particularly insightful question posed during a family dinner. They understood that curiosity was a flame that needed to be stoked, and they created an environment where asking questions was not just welcomed but encouraged. This familial support system was crucial in developing Samuel's confidence and willingness to explore uncharted territories in science.

Moreover, family outings to science museums and planetariums further fueled Samuel's fascination with the universe. These experiences were not just recreational; they were formative. Samuel was captivated by the exhibits on quantum physics, where concepts like wave-particle duality and uncertainty principles were presented in engaging ways. It was during one such visit that he first encountered the double-slit experiment, which would later inspire his own research. The experiment, which demonstrates the fundamental principles of quantum mechanics, can be summarized as follows:

$$\text{Intensity} \propto |\Psi|^2 \tag{3}$$

where Ψ is the wave function representing the probability amplitude of a particle's position. This realization of the dual nature of matter resonated deeply with Samuel, igniting a desire to delve deeper into the subatomic realm.

The influence of Samuel's family was also evident in their emphasis on humor as a coping mechanism. They often turned to comedy to lighten the mood during challenging times, teaching Samuel that laughter could coexist with serious pursuits. This blend of seriousness and humor became a hallmark of Samuel's approach to science. He learned to communicate complex ideas with a light-hearted touch, making science accessible and enjoyable for others.

In summary, the family influence on Samuel Park was profound and multifaceted. Their encouragement, support, and belief in his potential laid the foundation for his future innovations. Samuel's upbringing was characterized by a unique blend of scientific curiosity, resilience in the face of challenges, and the ability to find humor in the complexities of life. These elements combined to create a fertile ground for the growth of an innovative thinker who would one day unveil the secrets of the subatomic world.

Education and Early Scientific Interests

Samuel Park's educational journey was marked by a profound curiosity and a relentless pursuit of knowledge that began in his early childhood. Growing up in a household that valued education, Samuel was encouraged to explore a variety of subjects, but it was the mysteries of science that truly captivated him.

From a young age, Samuel exhibited a keen interest in the natural world. His parents often found him conducting experiments in the kitchen, mixing baking soda and vinegar to create fizzy eruptions, or observing the behavior of ants in the backyard. These early explorations laid the groundwork for his future scientific endeavors.

Elementary School: The First Glimmers of Interest

During his elementary school years, Samuel's passion for science was further ignited by a dedicated teacher, Ms. Thompson, who introduced her students to the wonders of physics through engaging demonstrations. One particularly memorable experiment involved a simple pendulum, which Samuel found fascinating. He learned that the period of a pendulum can be described by the equation:

$$T = 2\pi\sqrt{\frac{L}{g}} \qquad (4)$$

where T is the period, L is the length of the pendulum, and g is the acceleration due to gravity. Samuel was captivated by the idea that this simple formula could predict the behavior of a swinging object.

Middle School: A Passion for Physics

As Samuel progressed to middle school, his fascination with physics deepened. He eagerly participated in science fairs, showcasing projects that explored concepts like electromagnetism and energy transfer. One project involved constructing a simple circuit to power a light bulb, which Samuel explained using Ohm's Law:

$$V = IR \qquad (5)$$

where V is the voltage, I is the current, and R is the resistance. This project not only earned him accolades but also solidified his desire to pursue a career in science.

Samuel's middle school experience was also marked by a growing interest in quantum mechanics, a field that was still largely theoretical at the time. He devoured books about famous physicists like Albert Einstein and Niels Bohr, captivated by their groundbreaking ideas.

High School: The Turning Point

High school proved to be a pivotal time for Samuel. He enrolled in advanced placement courses in physics and mathematics, where he encountered more complex concepts such as wave-particle duality and the uncertainty principle. One particularly challenging topic was the concept of quantum superposition, which he learned could be illustrated by Schrödinger's equation:

$$i\hbar\frac{\partial}{\partial t}\Psi(x,t) = -\frac{\hbar^2}{2m}\frac{\partial^2}{\partial x^2}\Psi(x,t) + V(x)\Psi(x,t) \qquad (6)$$

where Ψ is the wave function, m is mass, and $V(x)$ is the potential energy. Samuel found himself enthralled by the idea that particles could exist in multiple states simultaneously, a concept that seemed to defy logic yet was fundamental to understanding the quantum realm.

During this time, Samuel also began to experiment with incorporating humor into his scientific presentations. He discovered that using comedic analogies helped his peers grasp complex concepts more easily. For instance, he likened electrons in an atom to hyperactive children bouncing around a playground, which not only drew laughter but also illustrated the unpredictable nature of electron behavior.

Extracurricular Activities: A Broader Perspective

Outside the classroom, Samuel sought opportunities to expand his scientific knowledge. He joined the school's science club, where he collaborated with like-minded peers on various projects. One memorable project involved building a model of the solar system, where Samuel took on the role of the lead designer. He ensured that the model accurately represented the relative distances and sizes of the planets, emphasizing the importance of scale in scientific representation.

In addition to his scientific pursuits, Samuel also participated in the drama club. This experience proved invaluable, as it honed his public speaking skills and taught him the art of storytelling. Samuel began to see the parallels between science and storytelling, recognizing that both fields required creativity and the ability to convey complex ideas in an accessible manner.

Conclusion: The Foundation for Future Discoveries

By the time Samuel graduated high school, he had developed a strong foundation in scientific principles and a unique approach to communicating complex ideas. His early education, characterized by curiosity, mentorship, and a willingness to embrace humor, set the stage for his future endeavors in the subatomic world. Samuel Park's journey was just beginning, but the seeds of innovation had already been sown, and he was ready to explore the depths of quantum mechanics with a blend of seriousness and levity that would define his career.

Challenges and Setbacks

Samuel Park's journey toward unraveling the mysteries of the subatomic world was fraught with challenges and setbacks that tested his resolve and determination. The path of an innovator is rarely linear; it is often marked by obstacles that can discourage even the most passionate individuals. For Samuel, these challenges were both personal and professional.

Navigating Academic Skepticism

From the outset, Samuel faced skepticism from the academic community. His unconventional ideas often clashed with established scientific norms. The prevailing belief in the scientific community was that breakthroughs in quantum mechanics required adherence to rigorous methodologies and a strict adherence to established theories. Samuel, however, was not one to be easily deterred. He believed that true innovation often requires stepping outside the boundaries of conventional thought.

One of the most significant challenges he faced was during his graduate studies when he proposed a radical hypothesis regarding quantum entanglement. He suggested that entangled particles could be manipulated using non-traditional methods, which contradicted the widely accepted principles of quantum theory. His professors viewed his ideas as naive, leading to numerous heated debates in the classroom. The equation that Samuel presented to support his hypothesis,

$$\psi(x_1, x_2) = \sum_{i=1}^{N} c_i \phi_i(x_1) \phi_i(x_2),$$

was met with skepticism. Many believed that the coefficients c_i could not be determined without relying on traditional quantum mechanics. This skepticism was a significant setback for Samuel, as it not only challenged his ideas but also affected his confidence.

Personal Struggles

Beyond academic challenges, Samuel faced personal struggles that compounded his difficulties. Growing up in a modest household, he often felt the weight of financial constraints. His parents, though supportive, could not provide the resources necessary for advanced scientific experimentation. Samuel's makeshift laboratory, which consisted of second-hand equipment and limited funding, became a symbol of both his resourcefulness and the limitations he faced.

The stress of financial instability took a toll on his mental health. He often found himself questioning whether he was on the right path. During this period of self-doubt, he turned to comedy as a coping mechanism. He began incorporating humor into his daily life, using it as a way to alleviate the pressure he felt. This approach not only provided him with a much-needed outlet but also allowed him to reframe his challenges as opportunities for growth.

Failures in Experimentation

As Samuel delved deeper into his research, he encountered numerous failures in his experiments. One of his early attempts to create a prototype for a quantum microscope resulted in a catastrophic malfunction. The apparatus, which was meant to visualize subatomic particles, exploded during a critical test run, scattering glass and components across his laboratory. The incident not only set back his research timeline but also damaged his reputation among his peers.

However, Samuel viewed this failure as a learning experience. He meticulously documented the failure, analyzing the causes in detail. He recognized that the explosion was due to an oversight in the calibration of the laser system, which he had designed based on his own untested theories. This realization led him to adopt a more methodical approach in future experiments, emphasizing the importance of rigorous testing and validation.

Isolation and Loneliness

The pursuit of groundbreaking discoveries often leads to isolation. Samuel found himself increasingly distanced from his peers, who were either unwilling or unable to embrace his unconventional methods. The loneliness of his journey was palpable; he frequently worked late into the night, surrounded by the silence of his laboratory.

In moments of solitude, Samuel reflected on the sacrifices he had made in pursuit of his dreams. He missed social gatherings and the camaraderie of his fellow students. This isolation, however, fueled his determination. He began to see himself as a pioneer, someone who was willing to venture into uncharted territories for the sake of scientific advancement.

Resilience and Growth

Despite the myriad challenges he faced, Samuel's resilience shone through. Each setback became a stepping stone toward his ultimate goal. He learned to embrace failure as an integral part of the scientific process. Samuel's ability to adapt and grow from his experiences was a testament to his character.

As he navigated the complexities of his research, he began to cultivate a network of like-minded individuals who shared his passion for innovation. These relationships provided him with the support and encouragement he needed to persevere. Samuel's journey was no longer a solitary endeavor; he was part of a community of thinkers who challenged the status quo.

In conclusion, Samuel Park's path to becoming a pioneer in subatomic discoveries was marked by challenges and setbacks that tested his resolve. From navigating academic skepticism to overcoming personal struggles and failures in experimentation, each obstacle contributed to his growth as a scientist. Through resilience and a willingness to embrace humor, Samuel transformed his challenges into opportunities, laying the foundation for his future breakthroughs in the subatomic world.

The Dream of Discovering the Subatomic World

Samuel Park's fascination with the subatomic world was not merely a passing interest; it was a profound dream that shaped his entire life. This dream was fueled by a combination of childhood curiosity, early exposure to scientific principles, and the relentless pursuit of knowledge. The subatomic realm, which includes particles such as electrons, protons, and neutrons, is governed by the laws of quantum mechanics, a field that Samuel would later come to master.

The Allure of Quantum Mechanics

Quantum mechanics, the branch of physics that deals with the behavior of matter and energy at the smallest scales, is characterized by phenomena that defy classical intuition. For Samuel, the allure of this field lay in its paradoxes and mysteries. He often pondered questions such as:

$$E = mc^2 \tag{7}$$

This equation, formulated by Albert Einstein, illustrates the relationship between energy (E) and mass (m), with c representing the speed of light in a vacuum. It was a cornerstone in understanding the fundamental nature of matter and energy, which would later inspire Samuel's own explorations.

Challenges in Understanding the Subatomic World

However, the journey to uncover the secrets of the subatomic world was fraught with challenges. Samuel faced numerous obstacles, including the abstract nature of quantum theory, which often left even seasoned physicists scratching their heads. Concepts such as wave-particle duality and quantum entanglement seemed almost magical. For example, the wave-particle duality of light, illustrated by the famous double-slit experiment, demonstrated that light can exhibit both wave-like and particle-like properties depending on how it is observed.

$$P(x) = |\psi(x)|^2 \tag{8}$$

In this equation, $P(x)$ represents the probability density of finding a particle at position x, while $\psi(x)$ is the wave function, which encodes all the information about the system. This duality was a source of both inspiration and frustration for Samuel as he sought to grasp the underlying principles governing the subatomic world.

The Role of Imagination in Scientific Discovery

Samuel believed that imagination played a crucial role in scientific discovery. He often recalled how, as a child, he would daydream about the invisible world that existed beyond the limits of human perception. This imaginative capacity allowed him to visualize complex concepts and formulate hypotheses that would later become the foundation of his groundbreaking work.

One of the most significant challenges in quantum mechanics is the concept of superposition, where a particle can exist in multiple states simultaneously until it is observed. Samuel found this concept both perplexing and fascinating. He often likened it to a comedic scenario, where a character could be in two places at once, leading to humorous misunderstandings and unexpected outcomes.

The Influence of Scientific Pioneers

Samuel drew inspiration from the works of pioneering physicists such as Niels Bohr and Richard Feynman, who made significant contributions to the understanding of atomic and subatomic phenomena. Bohr's model of the atom, which introduced the idea of quantized energy levels, provided a framework for Samuel's early studies.

Feynman's path integral formulation of quantum mechanics, which offers a way to calculate the probability of a particle's path by considering all possible paths, resonated deeply with Samuel's imaginative approach to science. Feynman's ability to communicate complex ideas with humor and clarity served as a guiding light for Samuel, who aimed to do the same in his own work.

The Vision of a Quantum Future

As Samuel progressed through his education, he became increasingly aware of the potential applications of quantum mechanics in technology and communication. The dream of discovering the subatomic world was not just an academic pursuit for him; it was a vision of a future where quantum technologies could revolutionize industries and improve the quality of life.

For instance, Samuel was particularly intrigued by the concept of quantum computing, which leverages the principles of superposition and entanglement to perform calculations at unprecedented speeds. He envisioned a world where complex problems, such as drug discovery and climate modeling, could be solved in a fraction of the time it currently takes.

$$Q = \frac{1}{2}mv^2 \tag{9}$$

This equation, representing kinetic energy, served as a reminder of the fundamental principles of physics that underlie all technological advancements. Samuel's dream was to harness these principles to create tools that could unlock the mysteries of the universe.

The Intersection of Science and Humor

In his pursuit of the subatomic world, Samuel also recognized the power of humor in science. He believed that making complex scientific concepts accessible through comedy could inspire a new generation of scientists and innovators. Samuel often incorporated comedic elements into his presentations, using light-hearted analogies to explain intricate theories.

For example, he would compare quantum entanglement to a pair of socks that, once separated, somehow still knew each other's whereabouts, regardless of the distance between them. This playful analogy not only entertained his audience but also helped demystify a complex topic.

Conclusion: A Dream Realized

Ultimately, Samuel Park's dream of discovering the subatomic world was a journey of curiosity, creativity, and resilience. It was a dream that propelled him to challenge conventional wisdom, embrace the unknown, and inspire others to explore the wonders of science. As he stood on the brink of his first major breakthrough, he reflected on the countless hours spent pondering the nature of reality and the joy of uncovering the secrets that lay beneath the surface.

In the words of Samuel himself, "The subatomic world is like a cosmic joke waiting to be unraveled, and I'm just the punchline waiting to be delivered." With this spirit, he embarked on a path that would not only change the course of his life but also the future of scientific inquiry itself.

The Spark of Inspiration

A Chance Encounter with a Brilliant Scientist

Dr. Elizabeth Reynolds: The Mentorship Begins

In the world of science, mentorship can often be the catalyst for innovation and breakthroughs. For Samuel Park, this pivotal role was played by none other than Dr. Elizabeth Reynolds, a distinguished physicist renowned for her work in quantum mechanics. The moment Samuel met Dr. Reynolds was not just a chance encounter; it was the spark that ignited his passion for the subatomic world.

A Serendipitous Meeting

Samuel's first encounter with Dr. Reynolds took place during a science fair at his university. As he presented his project on the principles of quantum superposition, he noticed a distinguished woman observing him intently. With her sharp gaze and an air of curiosity, Dr. Reynolds approached him after his presentation.

"Young man," she said, "do you understand the implications of what you've just described? The idea that particles can exist in multiple states simultaneously is not just theoretical; it's a window into the very fabric of reality."

Samuel, taken aback, stammered, "I—uh, I think so, but I'm still trying to wrap my head around it."

Dr. Reynolds smiled, recognizing the spark of curiosity in his eyes. "Curiosity is the first step towards discovery. Let's explore this together."

The Mentorship Begins

From that day forward, Dr. Reynolds became a mentor to Samuel, guiding him through the complexities of quantum mechanics. She introduced him to the foundational principles of quantum theory, emphasizing the importance of understanding both the mathematics and the philosophy behind it.

$$\Psi(x,t) = \sum_n c_n \phi_n(x) e^{-iE_n t/\hbar} \qquad (10)$$

In this equation, $\Psi(x,t)$ represents the wave function of a quantum system, while $\phi_n(x)$ are the eigenstates, E_n are the corresponding energy levels, and $\hbar$ is the reduced Planck's constant. Dr. Reynolds often emphasized that each term in this equation was not just a mathematical representation but a glimpse into the nature of reality itself.

Encouragement and Challenges

Dr. Reynolds encouraged Samuel to question everything, instilling in him a sense of wonder and skepticism that is crucial for any scientist. She often recounted her own challenges in the field, particularly how she had to navigate a male-dominated environment where her ideas were frequently dismissed.

"Science is not just about finding answers," she would say. "It's about asking the right questions and being brave enough to stand by your convictions, even when the world tells you otherwise."

This encouragement proved invaluable when Samuel faced criticism from his peers for his unconventional ideas. He had proposed a new method for visualizing quantum states that deviated from established norms.

The Influence of Humor

One of the most significant aspects of Dr. Reynolds' mentorship was her unique approach to teaching complex concepts through humor. She often used comedic analogies to explain intricate theories, making them more accessible and memorable.

For instance, she would compare quantum entanglement to a pair of socks in a laundry basket: "Imagine you have two socks. You can't tell which is which until you pull one out. But once you do, you instantly know the state of the other sock, no matter where it is in the basket. That's quantum entanglement!"

This approach not only made learning enjoyable but also helped Samuel to think creatively about his research. He began to incorporate humor into his own presentations, engaging his audience while explaining complex ideas.

A Lasting Impact

As their mentorship deepened, Samuel began to realize that Dr. Reynolds was not just a teacher; she was a pioneer who had paved the way for future generations of scientists. Her work on quantum coherence and its applications in quantum computing would become foundational in the field.

In one of their discussions, she stated, "The future of technology lies in our ability to harness quantum mechanics. It's not just about understanding the universe; it's about using that understanding to innovate and improve lives."

Inspired by her vision, Samuel set his sights on making his own contributions to the field. Under her guidance, he began to explore the idea of developing a quantum microscope, a tool that would allow scientists to visualize subatomic particles in unprecedented detail.

Conclusion

Dr. Elizabeth Reynolds' mentorship was instrumental in shaping Samuel Park's scientific journey. Through her encouragement, humor, and profound insights into quantum mechanics, she ignited a passion within him that would lead to groundbreaking discoveries. Their relationship exemplified the power of mentorship in science, proving that the right guidance can transform curiosity into innovation.

As Samuel often reflected later in his career, "Meeting Dr. Reynolds was like discovering a hidden dimension in my understanding of science. It was the beginning of my journey into the quantum realm, where dreams and reality intertwine."

Fascination with Quantum Mechanics

Samuel Park's fascination with quantum mechanics began at an early age, ignited by a chance encounter with Dr. Elizabeth Reynolds, a prominent physicist known for her innovative approaches to the subatomic realm. This encounter would serve as the catalyst for Samuel's lifelong journey into the enigmatic world of quantum physics, a domain where classical intuition often falters and the bizarre becomes the norm.

Quantum mechanics, at its core, is the branch of physics that deals with phenomena at the atomic and subatomic levels. Unlike classical mechanics, which describes the motion of macroscopic objects, quantum mechanics introduces a set of principles that challenge our understanding of reality. One of the most fundamental concepts is the wave-particle duality, which posits that particles such as electrons exhibit both wave-like and particle-like properties. This duality is encapsulated in the famous double-slit experiment, where particles can create an interference pattern, suggesting they behave as waves when not observed.

$$P(x) = |\psi(x)|^2 \tag{11}$$

In this equation, $P(x)$ represents the probability density of finding a particle at position x, and $\psi(x)$ is the wave function describing the quantum state of the particle. Samuel was captivated by the implications of the wave function, particularly the idea that reality is fundamentally probabilistic rather than deterministic.

As Samuel delved deeper into quantum mechanics, he encountered the concept of superposition, which allows particles to exist in multiple states simultaneously until measured. This phenomenon is exemplified by Schrödinger's cat thought experiment, where a cat in a sealed box is simultaneously alive and dead until an observer opens the box and collapses the wave function.

$$\text{State} = \frac{1}{\sqrt{2}} \left(|\text{alive}\rangle + |\text{dead}\rangle \right) \tag{12}$$

Samuel's mind raced with the implications of such ideas. He pondered the philosophical questions surrounding observation and reality: What does it mean for something to exist? How does the act of observation influence the state of a system? These questions fueled his desire to explore the quantum world further.

Moreover, Samuel was intrigued by the principle of quantum entanglement, a phenomenon where particles become interconnected in such a way that the state of one particle instantly influences the state of another, regardless of the distance separating them. This was famously illustrated by the Einstein-Podolsky-Rosen (EPR) paradox, which challenged the completeness of quantum mechanics and led to debates about locality and realism.

$$|\psi\rangle = \frac{1}{\sqrt{2}} \left(|00\rangle + |11\rangle \right) \tag{13}$$

In this entangled state, the measurement of one particle's state will instantaneously determine the state of the other, a phenomenon that Einstein famously referred to as "spooky action at a distance." Samuel's fascination with entanglement was not merely academic; he envisioned its potential applications in quantum computing and secure communication, where information could be transmitted instantaneously across vast distances.

Samuel's determination to make breakthroughs in quantum mechanics was further fueled by the realization that the field was still ripe with unanswered questions and unexplored territories. He often reflected on the challenges faced by early quantum theorists, such as Max Planck and Niels Bohr, who laid the groundwork for modern physics amidst skepticism and resistance. Inspired by their resilience, Samuel adopted a mindset that embraced creativity and humor as essential tools in scientific exploration.

Incorporating a comedic style into his scientific endeavors, Samuel began to view quantum mechanics not just as a set of equations and principles but as a source of inspiration for storytelling. He believed that humor could serve as a bridge to make complex concepts more accessible to the public. By crafting narratives that intertwined scientific theories with lighthearted anecdotes, he aimed to demystify quantum mechanics and inspire curiosity in others.

Through his exploration of quantum mechanics, Samuel Park not only developed a profound understanding of the subatomic world but also cultivated a unique perspective that blended science and humor. This fascination would become the driving force behind his groundbreaking discoveries, as he sought to unveil the mysteries of the universe with both intellect and creativity.

Samuel's Determination to Make Breakthroughs

Samuel Park's journey into the realm of quantum mechanics was not merely a pursuit of knowledge; it was a relentless quest fueled by an insatiable curiosity and a profound determination to make groundbreaking discoveries. From an early age, he demonstrated an unwavering commitment to understanding the universe at its most fundamental levels, often immersing himself in scientific literature and engaging in discussions that challenged conventional wisdom.

The Drive for Innovation

At the core of Samuel's determination was a belief that traditional scientific approaches were often too rigid, stifling creativity and innovation. He was inspired by the notion that real breakthroughs often come from thinking outside the box. This perspective was influenced by his early encounters with the works of renowned physicists such as Richard Feynman and Niels Bohr, who emphasized the importance of imagination in scientific inquiry.

$$E = mc^2 \qquad (14)$$

This iconic equation, formulated by Albert Einstein, symbolizes the profound relationship between energy (E), mass (m), and the speed of light (c). Samuel understood that just as energy could be transformed into mass, ideas could be transformed into revolutionary scientific advancements through innovative thinking and determination.

Facing Adversity

Samuel's path was not without its challenges. As he ventured into the world of quantum mechanics, he faced skepticism from established scientists who adhered to traditional methodologies. Critics often dismissed his ideas as fanciful or impractical, yet Samuel remained undeterred. He viewed these challenges as opportunities to refine his hypotheses and bolster his resolve.

For instance, during his early experiments with quantum phenomena, Samuel encountered significant technical obstacles. His attempts to manipulate subatomic particles using conventional equipment often resulted in failure. However, rather than succumbing to frustration, he embraced these setbacks as learning experiences. He famously quipped, "If at first you don't succeed, you're probably working in quantum mechanics!" This humorous outlook allowed him to maintain a positive attitude in the face of adversity.

The Role of Collaboration

Recognizing that collaboration could enhance his research, Samuel sought out partnerships with like-minded individuals who shared his passion for innovation. One of the pivotal moments in his career was the serendipitous meeting with Dr. Elizabeth Reynolds, a distinguished physicist known for her groundbreaking work in quantum optics. Their collaboration proved to be a catalyst for Samuel's breakthroughs.

Together, they formulated a series of experiments aimed at exploring the enigmatic properties of quantum entanglement. Samuel's determination to push the boundaries of scientific understanding was evident in their research. He often stated, "Science is a team sport; the more minds you have, the more ideas you can generate." This collaborative spirit not only enriched his work but also fostered an environment where creativity thrived.

Innovative Experimentation

Samuel's determination manifested in his willingness to experiment with unconventional methods. He believed that true innovation required a departure from established norms. This belief led him to design a series of experiments that combined elements of art and science, illustrating his unique approach to research.

For example, in one of his notable experiments, Samuel created a visual representation of quantum wave functions using light and sound. By employing a combination of lasers and audio frequencies, he was able to visualize the otherwise abstract concepts of quantum mechanics in a tangible form. This innovative approach not only captivated audiences but also provided a fresh perspective on complex scientific principles.

$$\Psi(x,t) = Ae^{i(kx-\omega t)} \tag{15}$$

The wave function, denoted as Ψ, describes the quantum state of a particle in terms of its position x and time t. Samuel's artistic interpretation of this equation bridged the gap between science and creativity, demonstrating that breakthroughs often arise from the intersection of diverse disciplines.

The Impact of Humor

Incorporating humor into his scientific endeavors became a hallmark of Samuel's approach. He believed that laughter could serve as a powerful tool for engaging audiences and simplifying complex concepts. During lectures and presentations, he often used comedic anecdotes to illustrate the intricacies of quantum mechanics, making the subject matter more accessible to students and the general public.

For instance, Samuel would joke, "Why did the physicist break up with the mathematician? Because they had too many problems!" This light-hearted approach not only made his talks enjoyable but also encouraged a deeper understanding of the material. By fostering a positive and engaging atmosphere, Samuel inspired others to embrace their curiosity and pursue their own scientific aspirations.

Conclusion

Samuel Park's determination to make breakthroughs in quantum mechanics was characterized by his innovative spirit, resilience in the face of adversity, and the ability to inspire others through humor and collaboration. His journey serves as a testament to the idea that true innovation requires a willingness to challenge the status quo, embrace failures as learning opportunities, and foster a collaborative environment where creativity can flourish. As Samuel often reminded his peers, "In the world of science, the only limits are the ones we impose on ourselves."

The Influence of Steve Martin's Comedic Style

Samuel Park's journey into the realm of quantum mechanics was not solely defined by rigorous scientific inquiry; it was also significantly shaped by his appreciation for humor, particularly the unique comedic style of Steve Martin. Martin, a multifaceted entertainer known for his work as a comedian, actor, and writer, embodies a form of humor that resonates with intellect and absurdity, which Samuel found particularly inspiring. This section explores how Martin's comedic approach influenced Samuel's scientific thinking and communication.

A Blend of Absurdity and Insight

Steve Martin's humor often juxtaposes the absurd with profound insights, a technique that Samuel adopted in his scientific endeavors. Martin's ability to take mundane situations and infuse them with unexpected twists serves as a reminder that creativity can emerge from the most unlikely scenarios. For instance, in Martin's classic stand-up routines, he frequently employed the technique of misdirection, leading audiences down one path before delivering a punchline that challenged their expectations.

Samuel recognized a parallel in the scientific process: the journey of inquiry often leads to unexpected discoveries. He adopted this principle of misdirection in his research, encouraging himself and his team to explore unconventional hypotheses. By embracing the absurdity of certain ideas, Samuel fostered an environment where radical thinking could flourish.

The Art of Storytelling

In addition to misdirection, Martin's storytelling prowess profoundly influenced Samuel's approach to presenting complex scientific concepts. Martin's narratives often blend humor with poignant observations about life, allowing audiences to engage with deeper themes while being entertained. Samuel sought to emulate this balance in his own work, believing that effective communication of science required more than just data and equations; it required a narrative that could captivate and inspire.

For example, during a lecture on quantum entanglement, Samuel recounted a humorous anecdote about a misunderstanding he had with a colleague over the nature of particle interactions. By framing the scientific discussion within a relatable story, he made the intricate subject matter more accessible to his audience. This method not only engaged listeners but also allowed them to grasp complex ideas without feeling overwhelmed.

Humor as a Teaching Tool

Samuel also recognized the potential of humor as a pedagogical tool. Inspired by Martin's ability to simplify complex ideas through comedy, he integrated humor into his teaching methods. Research has shown that humor can enhance learning by increasing engagement and retention of information [1]. Samuel's lectures often included witty analogies and playful language, making challenging topics like quantum mechanics approachable for students.

For instance, when explaining the concept of superposition, Samuel likened it to a situation where one might be both excited and nervous about an upcoming event, capturing the essence of the phenomenon while evoking laughter. This approach not only made the material more enjoyable but also encouraged students to think critically about the implications of quantum theory.

The Role of Comedy in Scientific Discourse

In a field often perceived as serious and rigid, Samuel championed the incorporation of humor into scientific discourse, echoing Martin's belief that laughter can bridge gaps in understanding. Samuel organized conferences where scientists were encouraged to present their findings with a comedic twist, fostering an atmosphere of collaboration and creativity. These events became platforms for researchers to share their work in a manner that was engaging and memorable.

During one such conference, Samuel delivered a presentation on the challenges of particle detection while incorporating a series of comedic skits that illustrated the difficulties faced by researchers in a light-hearted manner. This approach not only entertained attendees but also sparked discussions about innovative solutions to common problems in the field.

Conclusion

The influence of Steve Martin's comedic style on Samuel Park's scientific journey cannot be overstated. By embracing absurdity, storytelling, and humor as integral components of his work, Samuel transformed the way science was communicated and understood. His unique approach not only made complex topics accessible but also inspired a new generation of scientists to think creatively and push the boundaries of innovation. As Samuel often remarked, "Science is not just about equations; it's about the stories we tell and the laughter we share along the way."

Bibliography

[1] Martin, R. A. (2007). *The Psychology of Humor: An Integrative Approach.* Academic Press.

The Unconventional Path

Breaking Free from Traditional Scientific Methods

Samuel's Radical Ideas and Unorthodox Approaches

Samuel Park's journey into the world of quantum mechanics was marked by a series of radical ideas that defied conventional scientific wisdom. His approach to understanding the subatomic world was not merely a matter of rigorous experimentation and theoretical analysis; it was a creative endeavor that blended science with art, humor, and an unyielding curiosity.

Theoretical Foundations

At the core of Samuel's radical ideas was his profound understanding of quantum theory, particularly the principles of superposition and entanglement. The principle of superposition states that a quantum system can exist in multiple states simultaneously until it is measured. This can be mathematically expressed as:

$$|\psi\rangle = c_1|0\rangle + c_2|1\rangle \quad (16)$$

where $|\psi\rangle$ represents the quantum state, and $|0\rangle$ and $|1\rangle$ are the basis states, with c_1 and c_2 being complex coefficients. Samuel's radical idea was to explore the implications of superposition not only in theoretical contexts but also in practical applications, such as quantum computing and cryptography.

Challenging Established Norms

Samuel's unorthodox methods often put him at odds with established norms within the scientific community. For instance, while most physicists relied heavily on mathematical rigor and empirical evidence, Samuel believed that creativity played an equally important role in scientific discovery. He often stated, "Science is like comedy; timing and delivery are everything." This philosophy led him to adopt a more experimental and playful approach in his research.

One notable example of his unconventional thinking was his development of the "Quantum Joke Theory," which posited that humor could serve as a means of understanding complex quantum phenomena. Samuel argued that just as a punchline brings together seemingly unrelated ideas, so too could quantum particles exhibit correlations that defy classical intuition. This theory was not merely a whimsical notion; it prompted a series of experiments where humor was used as a mnemonic device to help students grasp difficult concepts, leading to improved comprehension and retention.

Innovative Experimentation

Samuel's laboratory, often described as a "mad scientist's playground," was filled with a variety of unconventional tools and instruments. He utilized everyday objects, such as rubber bands and kitchen timers, to create analog models of quantum systems. For example, he devised a simple experiment to illustrate quantum entanglement using two entangled rubber balls. When one ball was squeezed, the other would respond simultaneously, regardless of the distance separating them. This tangible demonstration helped demystify the concept of entanglement for his students and colleagues alike.

In his pursuit of radical ideas, Samuel also embraced interdisciplinary collaboration. He frequently invited artists, comedians, and writers to his laboratory, believing that their unique perspectives could spark innovative solutions to scientific problems. This collaborative spirit culminated in the "Quantum Art Festival," where participants created visual and performance art inspired by quantum mechanics, further blurring the lines between science and creativity.

Facing Criticism

Despite his successes, Samuel faced significant criticism from the scientific establishment. Many of his peers dismissed his ideas as frivolous or unscientific, arguing that humor had no place in serious research. Samuel, however, remained undeterred. He often quipped, "If you can't laugh at quantum mechanics, you're not paying attention!" His resilience in the face of skepticism only fueled his determination to prove that unconventional approaches could yield meaningful insights.

One particular instance of criticism came when Samuel proposed a radical reinterpretation of the double-slit experiment. He suggested that the act of observation itself could be influenced by the observer's emotional state, a concept he dubbed "Emotional Quantum Mechanics." While this idea was met with skepticism, it sparked discussions that led to new avenues of research into the observer effect and consciousness in quantum theory.

Conclusion

Samuel Park's radical ideas and unorthodox approaches not only challenged the status quo but also inspired a new generation of scientists to think outside the box. His belief in the power of creativity and humor in science opened doors to innovative methodologies that transcended traditional boundaries. As he often reminded his students, "In the world of quantum mechanics, the only limits are those we impose on ourselves." Samuel's legacy as a pioneer of unconventional thinking continues to resonate, encouraging future innovators to embrace curiosity, creativity, and a touch of humor in their scientific endeavors.

Facing Criticism and Doubts from the Scientific Community

In the realm of scientific discovery, innovation often walks a tightrope between brilliance and absurdity. Samuel Park, with his radical ideas and unconventional methodologies, found himself teetering on this precarious edge. His approach to quantum mechanics was met with skepticism from established scientists who were accustomed to the rigidity of traditional scientific protocols.

The Nature of Scientific Critique

Criticism in science serves as a necessary mechanism to ensure that theories are rigorously tested and validated. The scientific community, composed of peer-reviewed journals and conferences, thrives on a foundation of skepticism. As Samuel embarked on his journey to challenge the status quo, he encountered a barrage of critiques that questioned not only his findings but also his methods.

One notable instance of criticism came from Dr. Harold Finch, a prominent physicist known for his staunch adherence to conventional quantum theories. In a public forum, Finch dismissed Samuel's early work on quantum coherence, stating, "This is not science; it's mere speculation dressed in the garb of quantum jargon." Such comments stung, but they also fueled Samuel's resolve to prove his critics wrong.

The Problem of Paradigm Shifts

Samuel's work represented a paradigm shift—a term popularized by Thomas Kuhn in his seminal book, *The Structure of Scientific Revolutions*. Kuhn posited that scientific progress occurs through a series of revolutions rather than a linear accumulation of knowledge. Samuel's radical ideas about quantum entanglement and his development of the Quantum Microscope challenged the existing paradigms of physics, leading to resistance from those who felt threatened by the implications of his work.

The equation governing quantum entanglement, known as the Einstein-Podolsky-Rosen (EPR) paradox, is given by:

$$\text{EPR:} \ \Psi_{AB} = \sum_i \alpha_i \psi_A^i \otimes \psi_B^i \tag{17}$$

where Ψ_{AB} represents the entangled state of two particles, and α_i are the coefficients that describe the probability amplitudes of the respective states ψ_A^i and ψ_B^i. Samuel's interpretations of this equation, which suggested practical applications in communication technologies, were met with skepticism, as established physicists struggled to reconcile their understanding of quantum mechanics with his groundbreaking assertions.

Examples of Resistance

The resistance Samuel faced was not limited to theoretical critiques. During a presentation at the International Quantum Mechanics Conference, Samuel unveiled his Quantum Microscope, which promised unprecedented clarity at the subatomic level. The audience, a mix of seasoned scientists and eager students, was divided. While some applauded his ingenuity, others, including Dr. Finch, raised their hands in objection.

"Can you quantify your claims?" Finch challenged. "Your results lack statistical significance and repeatability, two cornerstones of scientific inquiry." Samuel, undeterred, responded with a blend of humor and confidence, "Well, if laughter is the best medicine, then perhaps a little humor can help us see the universe more clearly!"

This incident highlighted a significant challenge in science: the balance between creativity and rigor. Samuel's unconventional methods often led to results that were difficult to replicate, a common criticism in the scientific community. The reproducibility crisis in science, as noted by the *Nature* journal, has led to a reevaluation of how experiments are conducted and reported.

Overcoming Doubts Through Resilience

Despite the skepticism, Samuel remained steadfast in his belief that innovation required risk. He sought out allies in the scientific community who were open to new ideas, such as Dr. Elizabeth Reynolds, who recognized his potential. Together, they published a series of papers that began to garner attention, slowly shifting the perception of Samuel's work.

In a pivotal moment, Samuel proposed a collaborative experiment to test his theories on quantum entanglement. By utilizing state-of-the-art technology and rigorous statistical analysis, he aimed to demonstrate the validity of his claims. The experiment, which involved entangled photons, yielded results that not only supported his hypothesis but also captivated the scientific community.

The equation governing the behavior of entangled particles is represented as:

$$\text{Bell's Inequality: } S = |E(a,b) + E(a,b') + E(a',b) - E(a',b')| \leq 2 \quad (18)$$

where $E(a,b)$ denotes the correlation function between measurements at different angles. Samuel's results exceeded the classical limit, providing strong evidence for his theories and silencing many of his critics.

Conclusion

Facing criticism and doubt is an inevitable part of the scientific journey, especially for those who dare to challenge established norms. Samuel Park's resilience in the face of skepticism not only propelled his career but also paved the way for future generations of scientists. His story serves as a reminder that innovation often requires a blend of courage, creativity, and a healthy dose of humor to navigate the complexities of the scientific landscape.

Simple Beginnings in His Makeshift Laboratory

In the early days of his scientific journey, Samuel Park found himself in a modest, makeshift laboratory that was a far cry from the sophisticated research facilities of established institutions. This humble space, located in the basement of his family's home, became the birthplace of many of his groundbreaking ideas and experiments. It was here that Samuel learned the true essence of innovation: that sometimes, the most profound discoveries emerge from the simplest of environments.

The Environment of Innovation

Samuel's laboratory was filled with an eclectic mix of second-hand equipment, repurposed household items, and an abundance of curiosity. He had transformed an old workbench into his primary workspace, cluttered with beakers, wires, and an array of scientific instruments that he had either salvaged or built himself. This environment fostered creativity, allowing Samuel to experiment freely without the constraints often found in formal research settings.

Challenges Faced

However, working in such a limited space came with its own set of challenges. One of the most significant issues was the lack of advanced equipment necessary for high-level quantum experiments. Samuel often found himself grappling with the limitations of his tools. For instance, he needed a particle detector to explore subatomic particles effectively. Lacking funds for sophisticated devices, he improvised by using a combination of a Geiger counter and homemade sensors to detect radiation, which he hoped could lead him to a deeper understanding of quantum phenomena.

$$\text{Detection Efficiency} = \frac{N_{\text{detected}}}{N_{\text{total}}} \tag{19}$$

Where N_{detected} is the number of particles detected by his makeshift apparatus and N_{total} is the total number of particles emitted. Samuel's determination to optimize this efficiency led him to countless nights of trial and error, often resulting in humorous mishaps that he later used as material for his comedic routines.

Innovative Problem Solving

Despite the obstacles, Samuel's ingenuity shone through. He applied principles of quantum mechanics to devise creative solutions to his problems. For example, while studying wave-particle duality, he constructed a simple double-slit experiment using a laser pointer and a piece of cardboard. This setup allowed him to visualize the interference patterns that were central to understanding quantum behavior.

$$I(y) = I_0 \left(\cos \left(\frac{2\pi d \sin \theta}{\lambda} \right) \right)^2 \tag{20}$$

Where $I(y)$ is the intensity of the light at a given point on the screen, I_0 is the maximum intensity, d is the distance between the slits, θ is the angle of observation, and λ is the wavelength of the light. This simple experiment not only solidified his understanding of quantum principles but also served as an engaging demonstration for his friends, blending science with humor.

Incorporating Comedy into Science

Samuel's makeshift laboratory became a sanctuary for both scientific exploration and comedic expression. He often invited friends over to witness his experiments, turning each session into a blend of education and entertainment. By explaining complex concepts through humorous anecdotes and relatable analogies, he made science accessible and enjoyable. For instance, he compared the behavior of electrons to that of a group of overexcited children at a birthday party, running around chaotically yet predictably.

The Role of Failure

In his early experiments, failure was a frequent companion. Samuel learned to embrace it, viewing each setback as an opportunity for growth. One notable incident involved an attempt to create a rudimentary quantum entanglement setup. After several weeks of preparation, he inadvertently caused a short circuit that left his laboratory in darkness. Instead of despairing, Samuel used this experience to craft a stand-up routine about the "perils of quantum experimentation," which resonated with both scientists and laypeople alike.

Conclusion

In conclusion, Samuel Park's makeshift laboratory was more than just a physical space; it was a crucible for innovation and creativity. The challenges he faced and the solutions he devised laid the groundwork for his future breakthroughs in quantum mechanics. By merging his scientific pursuits with a flair for comedy, he not only advanced his understanding of the subatomic world but also inspired those around him to appreciate the beauty of science, even in its most chaotic forms. This unique combination of perseverance, creativity, and humor would become the hallmark of Samuel's illustrious career, setting the stage for his remarkable contributions to the field of quantum research.

Incorporating Comedy into Scientific Research

In the realm of scientific inquiry, the pursuit of knowledge often appears as a solemn endeavor, marked by rigorous methodologies and serious discourse. However, Samuel Park, with his unique perspective, recognized that humor could serve as a powerful tool in the scientific arsenal. By weaving comedy into the fabric of scientific research, he not only made complex concepts more accessible but also fostered an environment conducive to creativity and innovation.

Theoretical Foundations

The integration of comedy into scientific research can be understood through several theoretical frameworks. One prominent theory is the *Incongruity Theory of Humor*, which posits that humor arises when there is a discrepancy between what is expected and what actually occurs. This theory resonates with scientific exploration, where hypotheses often lead to unexpected results. Samuel leveraged this incongruity by presenting scientific findings in a humorous light, allowing audiences to engage with the material more deeply.

Another relevant theory is the *Benign Violation Theory*, which suggests that humor occurs when a violation is perceived as benign. In the context of science, this could involve poking fun at the complexities or absurdities of scientific processes, thereby reducing the intimidation factor often associated with technical subjects. Samuel's comedic approach transformed potentially dry material into relatable narratives, making science approachable and enjoyable.

Challenges and Solutions

Despite its benefits, incorporating comedy into scientific research is not without challenges. One significant problem is the risk of oversimplification. When humor is used excessively, there is a danger that the essential scientific rigor may be diluted, leading to misunderstandings of critical concepts. Samuel navigated this challenge by ensuring that his comedic elements complemented rather than overshadowed the scientific content. He often employed analogies and metaphors that maintained the integrity of the science while making it entertaining.

For instance, while explaining the concept of *quantum superposition*, he might compare it to a cat being both alive and dead, referencing the famous Schrödinger's cat thought experiment, but adding a humorous twist: "It's like when you can't decide whether to go out or stay in—until you look in the mirror and realize you're just a cat in a box!" This approach allowed audiences to grasp the concept while eliciting laughter, thereby reinforcing retention.

Examples of Humor in Research

Samuel's innovative approach to humor in science manifested in various forms, including stand-up performances, public lectures, and educational videos. One notable example was his viral TED Talk titled *"Quantum Laughs: The Subatomic Comedy Hour"*, where he combined elements of stand-up comedy with explanations of complex quantum phenomena. By using puns and witty observations, he transformed the often intimidating subject of quantum physics into an engaging spectacle.

In one segment, he humorously illustrated the concept of *quantum entanglement* by likening it to a long-distance relationship: "You might not see your partner every day, but somehow, you know when they're in trouble—just like entangled particles that can affect each other instantaneously, no matter the distance!" This analogy not only entertained but also clarified the concept for a lay audience.

Impact on Scientific Discourse

The incorporation of comedy into scientific research has profound implications for the dissemination of knowledge. Samuel's approach helped break down barriers between scientists and the public, fostering a culture of openness and curiosity. By making science fun, he encouraged more individuals to engage with scientific topics, thereby enhancing public understanding and appreciation of science.

Moreover, humor can serve as a catalyst for collaboration among researchers. In an environment where laughter is encouraged, scientists may feel more comfortable sharing ideas and exploring unconventional solutions. Samuel often hosted informal gatherings dubbed *"Science Comedy Nights"*, where researchers could present their work in a light-hearted manner. These events not only promoted camaraderie but also sparked innovative ideas that might not have emerged in a traditional setting.

Conclusion

Incorporating comedy into scientific research, as exemplified by Samuel Park, represents a transformative approach to science communication. By leveraging humor, he not only made complex scientific concepts more accessible but also fostered a more inclusive and collaborative scientific community. As the boundaries between disciplines continue to blur, the integration of humor into science will undoubtedly play a crucial role in inspiring future generations of innovators to explore the wonders of the universe with both curiosity and joy.

$$\text{Humor} = \text{Incongruity} + \text{Benign Violation} \qquad (21)$$

The Subatomic World Unveiled

Samuel's First Major Breakthrough: The Quantum Microscope

The Genius Behind the Invention

In the realm of scientific innovation, few breakthroughs have had as profound an impact as Samuel Park's invention of the Quantum Microscope. This revolutionary device was born out of a confluence of Samuel's unique perspective on quantum mechanics, his relentless curiosity, and an unconventional approach to scientific inquiry.

The Quantum Microscope operates on the principles of quantum mechanics, particularly utilizing the phenomenon of wave-particle duality. This duality allows particles, such as electrons, to exhibit both wave-like and particle-like properties. Samuel's genius lay in his ability to harness this duality to enhance the resolution of microscopic imaging.

$$\lambda = \frac{h}{p} \tag{22}$$

Where:

- λ is the wavelength associated with the particle,
- h is Planck's constant (6.626×10^{-34} Js),
- p is the momentum of the particle.

Samuel realized that by using electrons, which have much shorter wavelengths than visible light, he could achieve a resolution that far surpassed traditional optical microscopes. This insight was critical, as it allowed for the visualization of structures at the atomic level, unveiling a subatomic world that had previously been obscured.

However, the journey to this invention was fraught with challenges. Samuel faced skepticism from established scientists who were entrenched in classical methods. They argued that the complexities of quantum mechanics made it impractical for everyday applications. Samuel countered these criticisms with a series of experiments that demonstrated the feasibility of his ideas.

One notable experiment involved using a beam of electrons to image a sample of graphene. Samuel meticulously prepared the sample and adjusted the electron beam's parameters, demonstrating that the Quantum Microscope could resolve individual carbon atoms within the graphene lattice. This was a pivotal moment, showcasing not only the microscope's capabilities but also Samuel's innovative spirit.

$$I = I_0 e^{-\alpha x} \tag{23}$$

Where:

- I is the intensity of the electron beam after traveling a distance x,
- I_0 is the initial intensity,
- α is the attenuation coefficient of the material.

This equation illustrated the importance of understanding material properties when utilizing electron beams for imaging. Samuel's ability to integrate theoretical knowledge with practical experimentation was a hallmark of his genius.

Furthermore, Samuel's approach was not solely technical; he infused his work with creativity and humor. He often remarked, "Why did the electron break up with the proton? It found someone more attractive!" This light-heartedness not only made his presentations engaging but also helped demystify complex scientific concepts for his audience. By incorporating humor, he bridged the gap between advanced scientific theories and public understanding, making his research accessible and relatable.

The Quantum Microscope's design also featured a novel feedback mechanism that adjusted the electron beam in real-time, optimizing image quality and resolution. This innovation stemmed from Samuel's interdisciplinary background, where he drew inspiration from fields such as computer science and engineering. His ability to think outside the box and integrate diverse knowledge domains was crucial in developing a device that was as much an engineering marvel as a scientific instrument.

In conclusion, the genius behind the Quantum Microscope was not merely in its technical specifications but in Samuel Park's holistic approach to science. His willingness to challenge conventions, embrace humor, and blend various fields of knowledge culminated in a groundbreaking invention that opened new frontiers in microscopy. This device not only transformed the way scientists explore the subatomic world but also exemplified the spirit of innovation that Samuel embodied throughout his career.

As we delve deeper into the implications of the Quantum Microscope in the next sections, it is essential to recognize that the true brilliance of Samuel Park lay in his ability to inspire others to dream big and think differently—qualities that will undoubtedly shape the future of scientific exploration.

Revolutionary Impact on the Field of Microscopy

The advent of Samuel Park's Quantum Microscope marked a significant turning point in the field of microscopy, fundamentally altering how scientists observe and interact with the subatomic world. Traditional microscopy, based on optical principles, faced inherent limitations due to the diffraction limit, which restricts the resolution that can be achieved with visible light. According to the Rayleigh criterion, the minimum resolvable distance d between two point sources is given by:

$$d = \frac{1.22\lambda}{NA} \qquad (24)$$

where λ is the wavelength of light used, and NA is the numerical aperture of the microscope objective. This limitation meant that structures smaller than approximately 200 nanometers could not be resolved, leaving a vast realm of the nanoscale world hidden from view.

Samuel Park's breakthrough came with the introduction of the Quantum Microscope, which utilized principles of quantum mechanics to bypass these limitations. By employing quantum entanglement and superposition, the Quantum Microscope could achieve resolutions beyond the classical diffraction limit. The key innovation was the use of entangled photons to illuminate samples, allowing for the detection of interference patterns that reveal details previously thought to be inaccessible.

Theoretical Foundations

At the heart of the Quantum Microscope's functionality is the phenomenon of quantum entanglement. When two photons are entangled, their states become interdependent regardless of the distance separating them. This allows for the simultaneous measurement of multiple properties of a sample, leading to enhanced imaging capabilities. The mathematical representation of an entangled state can be expressed as:

$$|\psi\rangle = \frac{1}{\sqrt{2}} \left(|0\rangle_A |1\rangle_B + |1\rangle_A |0\rangle_B \right) \tag{25}$$

where $|0\rangle$ and $|1\rangle$ represent the two possible states of the photons, and subscripts A and B denote the two entangled particles. This entanglement allows for a form of imaging known as quantum-enhanced imaging, where the quantum properties of light enable the detection of weak signals that classical light sources cannot resolve.

Addressing Existing Problems

Prior to the Quantum Microscope, researchers struggled with several significant challenges in microscopy. For instance, the phenomenon of photobleaching, where fluorescent molecules lose their ability to fluoresce due to prolonged exposure to light, severely limited the duration and effectiveness of imaging studies. The Quantum Microscope mitigates this issue by using a pulsed light source that minimizes exposure time while maximizing the intensity of the signal captured.

Moreover, traditional microscopy often suffered from noise interference, which could obscure critical details in the imaging process. The Quantum Microscope employs advanced algorithms that leverage quantum information theory to filter out noise, enhancing the clarity and quality of the images produced. This capability is particularly important in biological applications, where the ability to visualize cellular structures and processes in real-time can lead to groundbreaking discoveries.

Examples of Impact

The revolutionary impact of Samuel Park's Quantum Microscope can be illustrated through several key examples in various fields of research. In the realm of nanotechnology, researchers utilized the Quantum Microscope to visualize the arrangement of atoms in a graphene lattice, providing insights into its electronic properties and potential applications in next-generation materials. This level of detail was previously unattainable with conventional microscopy techniques.

In the biological sciences, the Quantum Microscope enabled scientists to observe live cellular processes at the molecular level, such as protein interactions and cellular signaling pathways. This real-time imaging capability has profound implications for understanding diseases at a fundamental level, potentially leading to novel therapeutic strategies.

Additionally, in the field of materials science, the Quantum Microscope facilitated the study of phase transitions in complex materials, allowing researchers to investigate phenomena such as superconductivity and magnetism with unprecedented precision. The ability to visualize these transitions at the atomic scale has opened new avenues for the design of advanced materials with tailored properties.

Conclusion

In conclusion, Samuel Park's Quantum Microscope has had a revolutionary impact on the field of microscopy, overcoming the limitations of traditional methods and opening new frontiers in scientific research. By harnessing the principles of quantum mechanics, Park has not only enhanced the resolution and clarity of microscopic images but has also addressed longstanding challenges such as photobleaching and noise interference. The implications of this technology are vast, influencing diverse fields from nanotechnology to biology and materials science. As researchers continue to explore the potential of the Quantum Microscope, it is clear that Samuel Park's contributions will resonate for generations to come, inspiring future innovations and discoveries in the subatomic realm.

Unveiling the Hidden Beauty of the Subatomic World

In the realm of quantum physics, the subatomic world has often been portrayed as a chaotic and unintelligible domain. However, Samuel Park's groundbreaking invention of the Quantum Microscope unveiled a hidden beauty that not only brought clarity to the complexities of this miniature universe but also transformed our perception of reality itself.

The Quantum Microscope: A Revolutionary Tool

The Quantum Microscope, a revolutionary advancement in microscopy, allowed scientists to observe particles at a scale previously deemed impossible. Traditional optical microscopes, limited by the wavelength of light, could only resolve structures down to approximately 200 nanometers. However, Samuel's innovation utilized principles of quantum mechanics, particularly wave-particle duality, to achieve resolutions down to the atomic level.

The fundamental equation governing the behavior of particles in quantum mechanics is given by the Schrödinger equation:

$$i\hbar\frac{\partial}{\partial t}\Psi(\mathbf{r}, t) = \hat{H}\Psi(\mathbf{r}, t) \tag{26}$$

where Ψ is the wave function of the system, $\hbar$ is the reduced Planck's constant, and $\hat{H}$ is the Hamiltonian operator. By manipulating these quantum states, Samuel was able to create a device that could visualize subatomic particles in a manner akin to a painter revealing the intricate details of a hidden masterpiece.

The Aesthetic of Quantum Fluctuations

One of the most astonishing aspects of the subatomic world is the phenomenon of quantum fluctuations. These fluctuations, which arise from the inherent uncertainty in the position and momentum of particles, can be mathematically expressed through Heisenberg's Uncertainty Principle:

$$\Delta x \Delta p \geq \frac{\hbar}{2} \tag{27}$$

where Δx is the uncertainty in position and Δp is the uncertainty in momentum. Samuel's Quantum Microscope allowed researchers to visualize these fluctuations, revealing a dynamic and ever-changing landscape of particles that seemed to dance in and out of existence.

Through his lens, particles appeared not merely as static entities but as vibrant actors in a cosmic ballet. This visualization inspired a new appreciation for the beauty of the quantum realm, where uncertainty and probability interweave to create a rich tapestry of existence.

The Artistic Representation of Quantum States

Samuel Park was not only a scientist but also an artist at heart. He believed that the aesthetic appeal of scientific discoveries could bridge the gap between complex theories and public understanding. By collaborating with visual artists, he produced stunning representations of quantum states, turning abstract concepts into tangible art.

For instance, the visualization of electron clouds around an atom, which can be described by the probability density function:

$$P(\mathbf{r}) = |\Psi(\mathbf{r})|^2 \tag{28}$$

SAMUEL'S FIRST MAJOR BREAKTHROUGH: THE QUANTUM MICROSCOPE

was transformed into intricate 3D models that depicted the swirling, probabilistic nature of electrons. These artistic renditions captivated audiences and sparked curiosity about the subatomic world, encouraging a broader appreciation for quantum mechanics.

The Impact on Scientific Communication

Samuel's emphasis on the beauty of the subatomic world significantly impacted scientific communication. He often incorporated humor into his presentations, using comedic analogies to explain complex quantum phenomena. For example, he likened quantum entanglement to a cosmic game of charades, where two particles could instantaneously share information regardless of the distance separating them.

This approach not only made the science more accessible but also engaged audiences, fostering a sense of wonder about the universe. His comedic style became a hallmark of his lectures, making the intricate details of quantum mechanics both understandable and entertaining.

Conclusion: A New Perspective on the Subatomic World

Through the lens of the Quantum Microscope, Samuel Park unveiled a hidden beauty within the subatomic world that had long been obscured by complexity and abstraction. By blending science with artistry and humor, he transformed our understanding of quantum mechanics, inspiring a new generation of scientists and artists alike.

The hidden beauty of the subatomic world is not merely in its mathematical elegance but also in its capacity to evoke wonder and curiosity. Samuel's legacy serves as a reminder that science, when presented with creativity and passion, can illuminate the darkest corners of our universe, revealing a breathtaking landscape that invites exploration and discovery.

Crafting Science Fiction Stories with a Comedic Twist

Samuel Park's journey into the subatomic world not only led to groundbreaking scientific discoveries but also inspired him to explore the realm of storytelling. Combining the complex theories of quantum mechanics with humor, Samuel found a unique voice in crafting science fiction narratives that captivated both the scientific community and the general public.

Theoretical Framework

The intersection of science fiction and comedy can be understood through the lens of several theoretical frameworks. One prominent theory is the **Incongruity Theory of Humor**, which posits that humor arises when there is a discrepancy between expectations and reality. In the context of science fiction, this can manifest in exaggerated scientific concepts or absurd scenarios that challenge the audience's understanding of the universe.

For instance, consider the equation for the energy of a photon:

$$E = h \cdot f \tag{29}$$

where E is energy, h is Planck's constant, and f is frequency. Samuel could create a narrative where a photon, personified as a stand-up comedian, travels through space delivering jokes about its own energy levels, playing on the absurdity of a particle trying to understand its place in the universe.

Challenges in Blending Genres

While the fusion of science fiction and comedy presents exciting opportunities, it also poses challenges. One significant problem is ensuring that the scientific concepts remain accessible while still being entertaining. Samuel often faced criticism from purists who believed that humor could undermine the seriousness of scientific discourse.

To address this challenge, Samuel employed the technique of **Explanatory Humor**, where he would introduce complex ideas through comedic analogies. For example, he might compare quantum entanglement to a pair of twins who can sense each other's thoughts, regardless of distance, adding a humorous twist by suggesting they are just really good at texting each other.

Examples of Comedic Science Fiction Stories

Samuel's most notable work in this genre includes a short story titled *"The Quantum Comedian"*, where a quantum physicist accidentally creates a parallel universe filled with alternate versions of himself—each with a different comedic style. One version is a slapstick artist, another a dry wit, and yet another a pun master. This narrative not only explores the multiverse theory but also highlights the diverse ways humor can be expressed.

In another example, *"Entangled Laughs"*, Samuel crafted a story where entangled particles communicate through a series of increasingly ridiculous jokes.

The climax of the story occurs when the particles realize they can influence the outcomes of experiments by simply telling the right punchline at the right moment, thus illustrating the bizarre implications of quantum mechanics in a light-hearted manner.

Impact on Science Communication

Samuel's approach to storytelling significantly impacted science communication. By infusing humor into his narratives, he made complex scientific ideas more relatable and engaging. This method not only entertained but also educated audiences about quantum mechanics and its implications.

For instance, during public lectures, Samuel would often incorporate excerpts from his stories, using them as a springboard to explain intricate theories. This technique not only retained the audience's attention but also fostered a deeper understanding of the subject matter.

Conclusion

Crafting science fiction stories with a comedic twist allowed Samuel Park to bridge the gap between science and the public. By leveraging humor, he transformed complex scientific concepts into accessible narratives that inspired curiosity and laughter. Samuel's unique storytelling style not only enriched his own scientific journey but also left a lasting legacy in the world of science communication, encouraging future innovators to embrace creativity and humor in their pursuits.

Through his work, Samuel demonstrated that the universe, while often unfathomable, can also be a source of endless amusement and inspiration.

The Race for the Nobel Prize

Recognition and Validation of Samuel's Contributions

Nominations and Initial Speculations

As Samuel Park's groundbreaking research began to gain attention in the scientific community, the buzz surrounding his work culminated in the first nominations for the prestigious Nobel Prize in Physics. This section explores the initial speculations about his candidacy, the criteria for such nominations, and the reactions from both supporters and skeptics within the scientific realm.

The Criteria for Nobel Nominations

The Nobel Prize in Physics is awarded to individuals who have made significant contributions to the field, often characterized by groundbreaking discoveries that advance our understanding of the universe. According to the Nobel Foundation, nominees are evaluated based on their originality, the impact of their work on the scientific community, and the potential for future advancements. The nomination process is shrouded in secrecy, with nominators required to maintain confidentiality, which adds an air of intrigue and speculation to the proceedings.

Samuel's Rising Star

Samuel's nomination came on the heels of his revolutionary development of the Quantum Microscope, which allowed scientists to observe subatomic particles with unprecedented clarity. This innovation not only transformed microscopy but also opened new avenues for research in quantum mechanics. The initial speculations surrounding his nomination were fueled by the excitement within the scientific community, as colleagues and mentors began to advocate for his recognition.

$$\text{Impact} = \frac{\text{Breakthroughs}}{\text{Traditional Methods}} \qquad (30)$$

The equation above illustrates Samuel's impact on the field. By breaking away from traditional methodologies, he achieved breakthroughs that redefined the limits of scientific observation. His work was not merely an incremental improvement; it represented a paradigm shift in how scientists could study the quantum realm.

Peer Reactions and Controversies

While many celebrated Samuel's achievements, skepticism lingered. Critics pointed to his unconventional methods and the role of humor in his scientific presentations as potential distractions from the seriousness of his work. Some established scientists questioned whether his comedic approach undermined the rigor of scientific inquiry.

A notable instance of this skepticism was voiced by Dr. Harold Jenkins, a prominent physicist who stated, "While humor has its place in science, we must ensure that it does not overshadow the gravity of our discoveries." This sentiment resonated with a faction of the scientific community that valued traditional forms of presentation and communication.

Conversely, Samuel's supporters argued that his ability to engage audiences through humor made complex concepts more accessible. They pointed to his presentations at conferences where he seamlessly wove in comedic elements to explain intricate theories, thereby broadening the appeal of quantum mechanics to a wider audience.

The Speculation Game

As the nomination deadline approached, speculation reached a fever pitch. Various scientific journals and media outlets began to publish articles discussing the likelihood of Samuel receiving the Nobel Prize. Some articles highlighted his groundbreaking work on quantum entanglement, noting its implications for future technologies, such as quantum computing and secure communication systems.

$$\text{Quantum Entanglement} \rightarrow \text{Secure Communication} \qquad (31)$$

The equation illustrates the potential real-world applications of Samuel's research. His work suggested that entangled particles could be used to create unbreakable encryption methods, revolutionizing data security.

The Role of Public Perception

Public interest in Samuel Park's work also played a crucial role in the nomination process. The media's portrayal of his journey—from a curious child to a pioneering scientist—captured the imagination of the public and the scientific community alike. His story was not just about scientific achievement but also about perseverance, creativity, and the importance of humor in overcoming challenges.

As the speculation grew, Samuel found himself at the center of a media frenzy. Interviews and features highlighted his unconventional approach to science, leading to a broader discussion about the nature of innovation. Some commentators suggested that his candidacy for the Nobel Prize might even inspire a new generation of scientists to embrace creativity and humor in their work.

Conclusion of Initial Speculations

In conclusion, Samuel Park's nominations for the Nobel Prize in Physics not only reflected his significant contributions to the field of quantum mechanics but also sparked a larger conversation about the evolving nature of scientific inquiry. The initial speculations surrounding his candidacy underscored the interplay between innovation, public perception, and the sometimes contentious nature of scientific discourse. As the world awaited the official announcement, the excitement surrounding Samuel's potential recognition only grew, setting the stage for what would be a historic moment in the realm of science.

Competing with Established Scientists

Samuel Park's journey toward recognition in the scientific community was not merely a personal odyssey; it was a battlefield of ideas, innovation, and occasionally, egos. As he made strides in the realm of quantum mechanics, he found himself in direct competition with well-established scientists whose reputations were built on years of rigorous research and groundbreaking discoveries. This section delves into the challenges Samuel faced while navigating the complex landscape of scientific competition, the theoretical implications of his work, and the strategies he employed to carve out a niche for himself.

The Landscape of Established Scientists

The scientific community often resembles a high-stakes arena where established scientists wield significant influence. These individuals, often referred to as "big names" in their fields, have the power to shape research agendas and funding opportunities. Samuel was acutely aware of the hurdles posed by their established authority. For instance, he was competing against luminaries such as Dr. Harold Finch, known for his work on quantum field theory, and Dr. Maria Chen, a pioneer in particle physics. Both were not only respected but also had extensive networks that provided them with access to resources and opportunities that Samuel, with his unconventional methods, lacked.

Theoretical Challenges

One of the primary theoretical challenges Samuel faced was the prevailing skepticism surrounding his radical ideas. In quantum mechanics, the concept of *superposition*—where particles can exist in multiple states simultaneously—was well-documented. However, Samuel proposed an extension of this principle, suggesting that it could be applied to larger systems, which some established scientists deemed implausible.

The mathematical representation of superposition is given by the equation:

$$|\psi\rangle = \sum_i c_i |i\rangle \quad (32)$$

where $|\psi\rangle$ is the state of the system, $|i\rangle$ represents the basis states, and c_i are the complex coefficients that determine the probability amplitude of the system being in state $|i\rangle$.

Samuel's hypothesis was that if superposition could be scaled, it might lead to breakthroughs in quantum computing and communication. However, critics argued that such a notion contradicted the *Copenhagen interpretation* of quantum mechanics, which asserts that particles do not have definite properties until measured. This foundational disagreement placed Samuel at odds with the conventional scientific narrative.

The Problem of Credibility

To further complicate matters, Samuel's unorthodox approaches often led to questions about his credibility. His makeshift laboratory, filled with repurposed materials and quirky inventions, was a stark contrast to the polished environments of his competitors. This disparity created an image of a maverick scientist, which, while appealing to some, also fueled skepticism among peers who valued traditional methodologies.

For example, during a conference presentation, Samuel unveiled his prototype of the *Quantum Microscope*, which he claimed could visualize particles at unprecedented resolutions. The audience, comprising seasoned physicists, was initially skeptical. They demanded empirical evidence and rigorous validation of his claims. Samuel responded by proposing a series of experiments to demonstrate the capabilities of his invention, showcasing his willingness to engage with the scientific process despite the doubts cast upon him.

Strategies for Success

In the face of such formidable competition, Samuel employed several strategies to distinguish himself and gain recognition. One of his most effective tactics was to leverage humor and storytelling to communicate complex scientific concepts. Drawing inspiration from Steve Martin's comedic style, Samuel infused his presentations with wit and charm, making his research more accessible and engaging.

For instance, during a pivotal conference, he opened his talk with a humorous anecdote about a failed experiment involving a cat and a quantum superposition demonstration. This light-hearted approach not only captured the audience's attention but also disarmed critics, allowing him to present his findings in a more favorable light.

Additionally, Samuel sought collaboration with other innovative thinkers who shared his vision. By forming alliances with like-minded scientists, he was able to amplify his voice within the community. These collaborations often resulted in joint publications that showcased the groundbreaking nature of his work, thereby enhancing his credibility and visibility.

The Role of Public Perception

Public perception also played a crucial role in Samuel's competition with established scientists. As media coverage of his work increased, so did interest from the public, which in turn attracted funding and support. Samuel recognized the importance of engaging with the media to share his discoveries and the implications of his research.

He often participated in interviews and public speaking engagements, using these platforms to explain his work in layman's terms. By demystifying complex scientific ideas, he not only garnered public interest but also positioned himself as a relatable figure in the scientific community. This strategy proved effective in countering the elitism often associated with established scientists.

Conclusion

In conclusion, Samuel Park's journey to recognition was fraught with challenges as he competed against established scientists. The theoretical debates surrounding his work, the credibility issues stemming from his unconventional methods, and the need to navigate the complex landscape of scientific competition all contributed to a formidable barrier. However, through humor, collaboration, and effective public engagement, Samuel was able to carve out a space for himself in the scientific community, ultimately leading to his recognition and success. His story serves as a testament to the power of innovation and the importance of resilience in the face of adversity.

The Announcement: Samuel Park's Triumph

The day of the announcement was one that Samuel Park had both anticipated and dreaded. The air was thick with excitement and tension as the scientific community gathered in the grand auditorium of the International Academy of Sciences. The room was filled with luminaries, each one eager to hear the results of the Nobel Prize deliberations. As Samuel sat among his peers, he felt a mixture of hope and anxiety; the culmination of years of hard work was about to be revealed.

The Build-Up to the Announcement

In the weeks leading up to the announcement, speculation ran rampant. Samuel's groundbreaking research on quantum entanglement had garnered attention not only for its scientific merit but also for its innovative approach. His ability to merge humor with complex scientific concepts had made him a popular figure in both academic circles and the media. This dual appeal was exemplified in his viral TED talk, where he used comedic analogies to explain entangled particles, likening them to "two best friends who can finish each other's sentences, even from across the universe."

The Nobel Committee had been particularly impressed by his ability to communicate complex ideas, a skill that was increasingly seen as essential in today's world. As Samuel prepared for the announcement, he reflected on his journey, the challenges he faced, and the moment he first grasped the implications of quantum entanglement.

RECOGNITION AND VALIDATION OF SAMUEL'S CONTRIBUTIONS

The Announcement

As the clock struck noon, the President of the Nobel Committee approached the podium. The audience fell silent, their collective breath held in anticipation. With a warm smile, she began, "It is my honor to announce the recipient of this year's Nobel Prize in Physics. This year's prize is awarded to a scientist whose work has not only expanded our understanding of the quantum realm but has also inspired a new generation of thinkers and dreamers. The Nobel Prize goes to... Samuel Park for his pioneering research on quantum entanglement!"

A wave of applause erupted in the auditorium, drowning out the President's voice. Samuel, overwhelmed with emotion, stood up, his legs momentarily unsteady. He made his way to the stage, his heart racing. The moment felt surreal; he had dreamed of this day since childhood, and now it was finally here.

The Acceptance Speech

As he took the microphone, the applause slowly subsided. Samuel smiled, his signature blend of sincerity and humor shining through. "Thank you, thank you! I'd like to thank the Nobel Committee for this incredible honor. I must admit, when I first started studying quantum mechanics, I thought I was just trying to understand the universe. I had no idea I'd end up in a room full of people who are just as confused as I am!"

Laughter rippled through the audience, breaking the tension. Samuel continued, "Quantum entanglement is a phenomenon that challenges our understanding of reality. It's like a cosmic connection that defies the laws of classical physics. If you think about it, it's a bit like a bad relationship—no matter how far apart you are, you still feel connected!"

His humorous analogies resonated with the audience, making complex theories more accessible. He explained the implications of his work, emphasizing the potential for advancements in communication technologies, cryptography, and even quantum computing.

$$\text{Entangled State: } |\psi\rangle = \frac{1}{\sqrt{2}} \left(|00\rangle + |11\rangle \right) \tag{33}$$

This equation represented the simplest form of an entangled state, where two particles are interconnected regardless of the distance separating them. Samuel elaborated, "This equation is not just a mathematical representation; it's a glimpse into the fabric of our universe. It shows us that at a fundamental level, everything is connected."

The Aftermath

Following the announcement, Samuel was inundated with interviews and invitations to speak at conferences around the world. His work was not only recognized for its scientific merit but also for its ability to engage the public. He became a beacon of hope for aspiring scientists, showing them that humor and science could coexist harmoniously.

One notable instance was his appearance on a popular late-night show, where he demonstrated quantum entanglement using a pair of rubber ducks. "Imagine these ducks are entangled," he said, tossing one across the stage. "No matter where I throw this duck, the other one will always know what's happening!" The audience erupted in laughter, and the segment went viral.

In the months following the award, Samuel established the Park Foundation for Scientific Advancement, aimed at fostering curiosity and creativity in science. He understood that the future of innovation depended on inspiring the next generation to dream big.

Conclusion

Samuel Park's triumph was not merely a personal victory; it was a moment that redefined the relationship between science and society. By embracing humor as a tool for engagement, he had opened the door for a new era of scientific communication. His journey from a curious child to a Nobel laureate was a testament to the power of perseverance, creativity, and the belief that even the most complex ideas could be made accessible through laughter.

As he looked out at the audience that day, Samuel knew that his work was just beginning. The secrets of the universe were still waiting to be unveiled, and he was determined to continue exploring them—one joke at a time.

Incorporating Stand-Up Comedy into Scientific Conferences

The intersection of science and humor may seem unconventional, yet Samuel Park's approach to integrating stand-up comedy into scientific conferences revolutionized the way complex ideas were communicated. This method not only made the content more accessible but also engaged audiences in a manner that traditional presentations often failed to achieve.

Theoretical Framework

The use of humor in communication is grounded in several theoretical frameworks. One prominent theory is the *Incongruity Theory*, which posits that humor arises when there is a discrepancy between what is expected and what occurs. In a scientific context, this can be particularly effective when presenting surprising results or counterintuitive findings. For instance, when discussing quantum entanglement, Samuel might say:

> "If you think your relationship is complicated, try explaining quantum entanglement to your spouse!"

This not only captures attention but also serves to simplify the concept by relating it to everyday experiences.

Another relevant theory is the *Benign Violation Theory*, which suggests that humor occurs when something that threatens the norms of society is simultaneously perceived as benign. In a scientific setting, this can be used to challenge established norms or controversial theories in a light-hearted manner. Samuel often utilized this theory to address contentious topics, stating:

> "You know, if Schrödinger's cat were alive today, it would probably still be in the box, contemplating whether or not to pay its taxes!"

Challenges and Considerations

Incorporating humor into scientific discourse is not without its challenges. One significant issue is the risk of oversimplifying complex topics. While humor can make science more relatable, it can also lead to misunderstandings. Samuel was acutely aware of this balance and often emphasized the importance of accuracy in his comedic narratives.

Moreover, the audience's reception of humor can vary widely based on cultural backgrounds, familiarity with the subject matter, and individual preferences. Samuel navigated this by tailoring his material to the specific audience at each conference, ensuring that humor enhanced rather than detracted from the scientific message.

Examples of Successful Integration

One notable instance of Samuel's comedic approach occurred during the prestigious International Quantum Physics Conference. Faced with a room full of esteemed physicists, he began his presentation with a humorous anecdote about his early experiments:

> "When I first attempted to build a quantum microscope, I accidentally created a device that only saw things in my fridge. Turns out, quantum mechanics and leftover pizza have more in common than I thought!"

This opening not only garnered laughter but also served as a segue into discussing the challenges of visualizing the subatomic world.

In another example, during a panel discussion on quantum entanglement, Samuel quipped:

> "Entangled particles are like that one friend who always knows what you're thinking, even when you're trying to keep it a secret. Trust me, I've tried!"

Such remarks served to demystify complex concepts, allowing the audience to grasp the essence of quantum entanglement without getting lost in the mathematics.

Impact on Audience Engagement

The incorporation of stand-up comedy into scientific conferences significantly increased audience engagement. Feedback from participants often highlighted how Samuel's humor transformed their experience from a potentially dry lecture into an interactive and enjoyable session.

According to a survey conducted post-conference, 87% of attendees reported that they felt more motivated to explore quantum mechanics after Samuel's presentation, attributing their enthusiasm to his unique blend of humor and science.

Moreover, Samuel's comedic style fostered a more relaxed atmosphere, encouraging questions and discussions that might not have occurred in a more formal setting. This dynamic not only enriched the discourse but also inspired collaboration among attendees, breaking down barriers that often exist in academic environments.

Conclusion

Incorporating stand-up comedy into scientific conferences represents a paradigm shift in how scientific knowledge is disseminated. Samuel Park's innovative approach demonstrated that humor can serve as a powerful tool for engagement,

...sion, and retention of complex scientific concepts. By embracing ...mor, Samuel not only entertained but also educated, leaving a lasting impact on the scientific community and inspiring future generations of scientists to communicate their ideas with creativity and wit.

classical channels, allowing him to perform a corresponding operation on his entangled particle to recreate the state of the original particle.

Samuel was particularly excited by the potential of quantum cryptography, where entanglement could be harnessed to create unbreakable encryption methods. The concept of quantum key distribution (QKD) relies on the principles of entanglement to ensure that any attempt at eavesdropping would disturb the system, alerting the communicating parties to the presence of an intruder.

Through his exploration of quantum entanglement, Samuel Park not only expanded his understanding of the phenomenon but also began to appreciate its profound implications for the future of technology. His journey was not without its challenges; he faced skepticism from traditionalists who clung to classical notions of reality. However, Samuel's determination to embrace the mysteries of the quantum realm fueled his innovative spirit and laid the groundwork for his groundbreaking discoveries.

In conclusion, Samuel's journey to understand quantum entanglement exemplified the delicate balance between theory and experimentation, intuition and mathematics. It was a journey marked by curiosity, resilience, and a relentless pursuit of knowledge, ultimately leading him to unravel the secrets of the universe and inspire future generations of scientists.

Implications for Communication and Technology

The discovery of quantum entanglement by Samuel Park has far-reaching implications for communication and technology, revolutionizing the way we understand information transfer at a fundamental level. Quantum entanglement, a phenomenon where particles become interconnected such that the state of one particle instantaneously influences the state of another, regardless of the distance separating them, presents a new frontier in secure communication and computational capabilities.

Quantum Communication

One of the most significant applications of quantum entanglement is in the realm of quantum communication. Traditional communication systems rely on classical bits, which can be easily intercepted or manipulated. In contrast, quantum communication utilizes quantum bits (qubits), which can exist in superpositions of states. This allows for the transmission of information in a manner that is inherently secure.

The principle of *quantum key distribution* (QKD) exemplifies this advantage. QKD allows two parties to generate a shared, secret random key that can be used for secure communication. The security of QKD is guaranteed by the laws of quantum mechanics, specifically the no-cloning theorem, which states that it is impossible to create an identical copy of an arbitrary unknown quantum state. This means that any attempt to eavesdrop on the communication will inevitably disturb the quantum states being transmitted, alerting the communicating parties to the presence of an intruder.

The most notable implementation of QKD is the BB84 protocol, developed by Charles Bennett and Gilles Brassard in 1984. In this protocol, Alice and Bob (the communicating parties) use polarized photons to encode bits. The security of the transmission can be mathematically expressed as:

$$E = 1 - \frac{S}{N} \tag{34}$$

where E is the error rate, S is the number of successfully transmitted bits, and N is the total number of bits sent. If the error rate exceeds a certain threshold, the key is discarded, ensuring that only secure keys are used for encryption.

Quantum Teleportation

Another groundbreaking application stemming from quantum entanglement is quantum teleportation. This process enables the transfer of quantum states from one location to another without moving the physical particle itself. Quantum teleportation relies on entangled particles shared between the sender and receiver, allowing for the instantaneous transmission of information.

The process can be described mathematically through the following steps:
1. **Preparation of Entangled State**: Two parties, Alice and Bob, share an entangled pair of qubits, denoted as $|\psi\rangle$. 2. **Measurement**: Alice performs a joint measurement on her qubit and the qubit she wishes to teleport, collapsing the state into one of the basis states. 3. **Classical Communication**: Alice sends the result of her measurement to Bob through classical channels. 4. **Reconstruction**: Bob applies a corresponding operation on his entangled qubit based on Alice's measurement result, resulting in the teleportation of the original qubit's state.

This process can be mathematically expressed as:

$$|\psi\rangle = \alpha|0\rangle + \beta|1\rangle \quad \text{with } \alpha, \beta \in \mathbb{C} \tag{35}$$

where $|\psi\rangle$ is the state being teleported. The implications of quantum teleportation extend beyond theoretical curiosity, with potential applications in quantum computing networks and secure data transmission.

Quantum Computing and Its Technological Revolution

The implications of Samuel Park's discoveries also extend into the realm of quantum computing, where entanglement plays a crucial role in enhancing computational power. Quantum computers leverage the principles of superposition and entanglement to process information in ways that classical computers cannot.

The computational advantage of quantum computers can be illustrated through algorithms such as Shor's algorithm, which efficiently factors large integers. The ability to factor large numbers has profound implications for cryptography, as many encryption systems rely on the difficulty of this task. Shor's algorithm operates in polynomial time, while the best-known classical algorithms operate in exponential time. This can be represented mathematically as:

$$T(n) = O(n^3) \quad \text{(Shor's Algorithm)} \tag{36}$$

versus

$$T(n) = O(e^n) \quad \text{(Classical Algorithms)} \tag{37}$$

where $T(n)$ is the time complexity and n is the number of digits in the integer being factored. The exponential speedup offered by quantum computing could render many traditional cryptographic methods obsolete, necessitating the development of new quantum-resistant algorithms.

Challenges and Ethical Considerations

Despite the exciting prospects of quantum communication and computing, several challenges remain. The implementation of quantum technologies requires significant advancements in materials science, error correction, and infrastructure. Quantum states are notoriously fragile, making them susceptible to decoherence and noise, which can degrade the quality of communication and computation.

Moreover, ethical considerations arise with the advent of such powerful technologies. The potential for misuse, particularly in terms of surveillance and privacy invasion, necessitates a robust framework for the ethical use of quantum technologies. Policymakers and scientists must collaborate to establish guidelines that ensure these innovations are harnessed for the benefit of society as a whole.

Conclusion

In conclusion, Samuel Park's exploration of quantum entanglement has opened new avenues for communication and technology, promising secure communication systems, revolutionary computing capabilities, and a deeper understanding of the universe. As we stand on the brink of a quantum revolution, it is essential to navigate the challenges and ethical considerations that accompany these advancements, ensuring that the future of technology is not only innovative but also responsible and equitable.

The Quest for Practical Application

The journey to transform theoretical discoveries into practical applications is often fraught with challenges and complexities. For Samuel Park, the understanding of quantum entanglement was not merely an academic achievement; it represented a pivotal moment in the quest for revolutionary technologies that could reshape communication, computing, and even the very fabric of reality as we know it.

Understanding Quantum Entanglement

Quantum entanglement is a phenomenon that occurs when particles become intertwined in such a way that the state of one particle instantaneously affects the state of another, regardless of the distance separating them. Mathematically, this can be expressed using the concept of a wave function, Ψ, which describes the quantum state of a system. For a system of two entangled particles, the joint wave function can be represented as follows:

$$\Psi_{AB} = \sum_{i,j} c_{ij} |a_i\rangle |b_j\rangle$$

where $|a_i\rangle$ and $|b_j\rangle$ are the states of particles A and B, respectively, and c_{ij} are coefficients that describe the probabilities of finding the particles in those states.

One of the most intriguing implications of quantum entanglement is its potential application in quantum communication and quantum computing. However, to harness this phenomenon, several theoretical and practical challenges must be addressed.

Challenges in Practical Application

1. **Decoherence** One of the primary challenges in utilizing quantum entanglement is decoherence, which occurs when the entangled particles interact

with their environment, leading to the loss of their quantum state. This phenomenon can be mathematically described by the Lindblad equation, which models the evolution of the density matrix ρ of a quantum system:

$$\frac{d\rho}{dt} = -i[H, \rho] + \sum_k \left(L_k \rho L_k^\dagger - \frac{1}{2} \{L_k^\dagger L_k, \rho\} \right)$$

where H is the Hamiltonian of the system, and L_k are the Lindblad operators that describe the interaction with the environment. Overcoming decoherence is essential for maintaining the integrity of quantum states during practical applications.

2. Scalability Another significant hurdle is scalability. While small-scale quantum systems have demonstrated entanglement, creating larger systems that can maintain entanglement over time and space remains a formidable challenge. For instance, the creation of a quantum network that spans vast distances requires not only the entanglement of particles but also reliable methods to distribute and manage these entangled states.

3. Error Correction Quantum systems are inherently susceptible to errors due to noise and decoherence. Implementing effective quantum error correction codes is crucial for ensuring the reliability of quantum communication and computation. One such example is the Shor code, which can protect quantum information by encoding it into a larger Hilbert space, thus allowing for the recovery of information even when some qubits are lost or corrupted.

Examples of Practical Applications

Despite these challenges, Samuel Park's work laid the groundwork for several promising applications of quantum entanglement:

1. Quantum Key Distribution (QKD) One of the most significant applications is Quantum Key Distribution, a method that allows two parties to share a secret key securely. The most famous protocol is the BB84 protocol, which utilizes the principles of quantum mechanics to ensure that any attempt to eavesdrop will disturb the quantum states being transmitted, alerting the parties involved. Samuel's research into entangled states provided insights into enhancing the security of QKD systems, making them more robust against potential attacks.

2. Quantum Teleportation Quantum teleportation is another groundbreaking application that Samuel Park explored. It allows for the transfer of quantum states from one location to another without physically transmitting the particle itself. This process relies on entangled particles and the phenomenon of classical communication. The mathematical representation of quantum teleportation can be summarized as follows:

1. Prepare an entangled pair of qubits, $|E\rangle = \frac{1}{\sqrt{2}}(|00\rangle + |11\rangle)$. 2. Alice measures her qubit and sends the result to Bob. 3. Bob performs a corresponding operation on his qubit to recreate Alice's original state.

This process highlights the potential for instantaneous communication across vast distances, a concept that Samuel believed could revolutionize information transfer.

3. Quantum Computing Lastly, quantum computing represents a frontier that Samuel Park passionately pursued. By utilizing quantum bits (qubits) that can exist in multiple states simultaneously due to superposition and entanglement, quantum computers can solve complex problems much faster than classical computers. Samuel's work contributed to the development of quantum algorithms, such as Grover's algorithm for searching unsorted databases, which operates in $O(\sqrt{N})$ time compared to the classical $O(N)$ time complexity.

Conclusion

The quest for practical applications of quantum entanglement is a journey marked by both promise and challenge. Samuel Park's contributions have not only advanced our understanding of this enigmatic phenomenon but have also inspired a new generation of scientists to explore its potential. As we continue to navigate the complexities of quantum mechanics, the integration of theory and practice remains crucial in unlocking the full capabilities of quantum technologies. Samuel's legacy in this field serves as a testament to the importance of perseverance, creativity, and the belief that the impossible can become possible through innovation and collaboration.

Using Comedy to Explain Complex Concepts to the Public

In an era where scientific literacy is paramount, the ability to convey complex ideas in an engaging manner has become increasingly important. Samuel Park recognized this need early in his career, understanding that humor could serve as a bridge between the intricate world of quantum mechanics and the general public.

This section explores the theories behind using comedy as a pedagogical tool, the challenges faced, and examples of how Samuel effectively utilized humor to demystify subatomic phenomena.

Theoretical Foundation of Humor in Education

The incorporation of humor into education is supported by several theories. One prominent theory is the *Incongruity Theory*, which posits that humor arises when there is a discrepancy between what is expected and what occurs. This unexpected twist can lead to amusement, making the material more memorable. In the context of science education, when Samuel presented a complex concept, such as quantum entanglement, through a comedic lens, he created a cognitive dissonance that engaged his audience.

Another relevant theory is the *Relief Theory*, which suggests that humor serves as a mechanism to relieve psychological tension. Scientific topics can often induce anxiety or confusion; by introducing humor, Samuel alleviated these feelings, allowing his audience to approach the material with a lighter heart. This technique not only made the information more accessible but also fostered a positive learning environment.

Challenges in Using Comedy

While humor can be a powerful educational tool, it is not without its challenges. One primary concern is the risk of oversimplification. In his enthusiasm to make quantum mechanics approachable, Samuel had to be careful not to dilute the scientific content. For instance, when explaining the concept of *superposition*, he might joke, "It's like being in two places at once—something my mother always accused me of when I was late for dinner!" While humorous, such statements must be followed by a clear and accurate explanation to ensure understanding.

Another challenge is the potential for misunderstanding. Not all audiences share the same cultural references or sense of humor. Samuel had to tailor his comedic approach to suit diverse audiences, which required a keen awareness of context. For example, while a joke about Schrödinger's cat might resonate with a group of physicists, it could fall flat in a general audience unfamiliar with the concept.

Practical Examples of Humor in Science Communication

Samuel Park's ability to blend humor with science was exemplified in his public lectures and outreach programs. One memorable instance occurred during a TED

Talk, where he used a series of comedic analogies to explain *quantum tunneling*. He likened it to "a cat trying to sneak out of a closed door—sometimes it just pops through without opening it!" This analogy not only captured the audience's attention but also provided a relatable image of a complex phenomenon.

Another effective technique was his use of comedic skits in educational videos. In one video, Samuel donned a lab coat and played the role of a mad scientist, humorously exaggerating the quirks of quantum physics. By dramatizing scenarios such as the uncertainty principle, he transformed potentially dry material into an entertaining narrative. The skits concluded with a straightforward explanation of the concepts, reinforcing the educational message while keeping the audience engaged.

Conclusion: The Impact of Humor on Science Communication

Samuel Park's innovative approach to science communication through comedy highlights the profound impact humor can have on understanding complex concepts. By leveraging the theoretical foundations of humor and addressing the challenges involved, he successfully bridged the gap between the scientific community and the public. His legacy serves as a reminder that laughter not only enriches our lives but also enhances our ability to learn and understand the intricate workings of the universe.

In conclusion, using comedy to explain complex scientific ideas is not merely a novel approach; it is a vital strategy for fostering curiosity and promoting scientific literacy. Samuel Park's journey illustrates that embracing humor can inspire future generations to explore the wonders of science with enthusiasm and joy.

Samuel's Legacy

Inspiring the Next Generation of Innovators

Establishing the Park Foundation for Scientific Advancement

In the wake of his groundbreaking discoveries, Samuel Park recognized the necessity of nurturing the next generation of scientists who would continue to push the boundaries of knowledge and innovation. Thus, he established the Park Foundation for Scientific Advancement, a non-profit organization dedicated to supporting scientific research, education, and outreach. The foundation aimed to create a vibrant ecosystem where curiosity and creativity could flourish, much like the quantum particles Samuel had dedicated his life to studying.

Vision and Mission

The vision of the Park Foundation was clear: to empower young scientists and innovators by providing them with the resources, mentorship, and opportunities they need to explore the frontiers of science. The mission statement emphasized the importance of interdisciplinary collaboration, creativity, and the integration of humor into the scientific discourse, reflecting Samuel's own approach to science.

> *"To inspire, educate, and empower the next generation of innovators through accessible resources, mentorship, and a commitment to creativity in scientific exploration."*

Programs and Initiatives

The foundation launched several key programs to achieve its mission:

- **Scholarship Programs:** The Park Foundation offered scholarships to students pursuing degrees in science, technology, engineering, and mathematics (STEM). These scholarships aimed to alleviate financial burdens and encourage diverse participation in scientific fields.

- **Mentorship Initiatives:** Samuel personally mentored selected students and young scientists, providing guidance on research projects and career development. The foundation also paired students with established scientists across various disciplines to foster networking and collaboration.

- **Workshops and Seminars:** Regular workshops were organized to teach practical skills and innovative techniques in research. These events often included guest speakers from various fields, including comedy, to illustrate the importance of creativity in scientific thinking.

- **Public Outreach Programs:** To engage the community and inspire interest in science, the foundation organized science fairs, public lectures, and interactive demonstrations. Samuel often incorporated humor into these events, making complex scientific concepts accessible and enjoyable for all ages.

- **Research Grants:** The foundation provided grants for innovative research projects, particularly those that explored unconventional ideas or interdisciplinary approaches. This initiative encouraged scientists to think outside the box, echoing Samuel's own journey through the scientific landscape.

Impact on the Scientific Community

The establishment of the Park Foundation had a profound impact on the scientific community. By fostering a culture of collaboration and creativity, the foundation contributed to a new generation of thinkers who approached problems with fresh perspectives. For example, one of the foundation's scholarship recipients, Dr. Maya Chen, developed a novel method for visualizing quantum entanglement, which garnered international attention and led to significant advancements in quantum computing.

The foundation's emphasis on humor in science also reshaped how scientific communication occurred. Workshops on using comedic techniques in presentations became popular, as scientists learned to engage audiences more effectively. This approach not only made science more relatable but also encouraged a broader appreciation for the subject.

Challenges and Solutions

Despite its successes, the Park Foundation faced challenges. Securing funding in a competitive landscape was a constant struggle. To address this, Samuel leveraged his network of influential scientists and philanthropists, hosting fundraising events that highlighted the foundation's achievements and future goals.

Additionally, the foundation encountered skepticism from traditionalists in the scientific community who questioned the integration of humor into serious scientific discourse. Samuel addressed these concerns by showcasing successful case studies where humor had enhanced understanding and engagement. By promoting a culture of openness and experimentation, the foundation gradually gained acceptance for its unconventional methods.

Future Aspirations

Looking ahead, the Park Foundation aims to expand its reach globally, establishing partnerships with international institutions to promote scientific literacy and innovation. The foundation envisions a future where every curious mind, regardless of background, has the opportunity to explore the wonders of science.

In conclusion, the establishment of the Park Foundation for Scientific Advancement marked a significant milestone in Samuel Park's legacy. By nurturing young talent, promoting interdisciplinary collaboration, and embracing creativity and humor, the foundation continues to inspire a new generation of innovators ready to tackle the challenges of the future. Samuel's belief that science should be accessible and enjoyable remains at the heart of the foundation's mission, ensuring that the spirit of inquiry and discovery lives on.

Mentoring Future Scientists and Encouraging Curiosity

Samuel Park understood that the key to fostering innovation lies in nurturing the curiosity of young minds. His approach to mentoring future scientists was not merely about imparting knowledge; it was about igniting a passion for discovery and encouraging the questioning spirit that drives scientific inquiry.

The Importance of Mentorship

Mentorship plays a crucial role in the development of future scientists. A study published in the journal *Science* indicated that students with mentors are more likely to pursue careers in science, technology, engineering, and mathematics (STEM) fields [?]. Samuel recognized that his own journey was significantly influenced by his mentor, Dr. Elizabeth Reynolds. Inspired by her guidance, he sought to replicate that experience for others, understanding that mentorship could bridge the gap between theoretical knowledge and practical application.

Creating an Engaging Learning Environment

To cultivate curiosity, Samuel established a series of workshops and summer camps through the Park Foundation. These programs focused on hands-on experiments and real-world applications of scientific principles. For instance, one particularly popular workshop involved building simple quantum devices using everyday materials. Participants were challenged to create a basic version of a quantum eraser, demonstrating the principles of quantum mechanics in an accessible manner.

The equation governing the quantum eraser experiment can be expressed as follows:

$$P = \frac{1}{2}\left(1 + \cos\left(\frac{\Delta\phi}{\hbar}\right)\right) \quad (38)$$

where P is the probability of detecting a photon in a given state, $\Delta\phi$ is the phase difference, and $\hbar$ is the reduced Planck's constant. By allowing students to manipulate variables and observe outcomes, Samuel encouraged them to think critically about the implications of quantum mechanics.

Encouraging Questions and Exploration

Samuel fostered an environment where questioning was not only accepted but celebrated. He often quoted his favorite comedian, Steve Martin, saying, "A day without laughter is a day wasted," and adapted this philosophy to science: "A day without questions is a day wasted." He encouraged students to ask "why" and "how," leading them to explore deeper into scientific concepts.

For example, during a discussion on quantum entanglement, he prompted students with questions such as:

- What happens to entangled particles when they are separated?
- How could this phenomenon revolutionize communication technology?

This questioning technique not only stimulated intellectual curiosity but also led to spirited debates among students, fostering a community of inquiry.

Utilizing Humor in Science Education

Incorporating humor into science education was one of Samuel's most innovative strategies. He believed that laughter could reduce anxiety associated with complex topics and make learning more enjoyable. To illustrate this point, he often used humorous analogies to explain complicated theories.

For instance, when discussing the concept of superposition in quantum mechanics, he would say, "Imagine you're trying to decide between pizza and sushi for dinner. Until you open the menu, you're in a state of superposition—both options are on the table until you make a choice!" This light-hearted approach helped demystify abstract concepts and made them relatable to students.

Real-World Applications and Problem-Solving

Samuel emphasized the importance of applying theoretical knowledge to real-world problems. He encouraged students to identify challenges in their communities and propose scientific solutions. One notable project involved students designing a low-cost water purification system using principles of physics and chemistry.

The students utilized the following equation to calculate the efficiency of their system:

$$E = \frac{V_{clean}}{V_{total}} \times 100 \qquad (39)$$

where E is the efficiency percentage, V_{clean} is the volume of purified water, and V_{total} is the total volume of water processed. This project not only provided practical experience but also instilled a sense of responsibility and purpose in the students.

Conclusion

Through his mentorship, Samuel Park not only inspired a new generation of scientists but also instilled a sense of wonder and curiosity that is essential for innovation. By creating engaging learning environments, encouraging questions, utilizing humor, and emphasizing real-world applications, he laid the groundwork for a future where scientific inquiry thrives. Samuel's legacy as a mentor is a testament to the power of curiosity in driving the next wave of scientific discovery.

Leaving a Lasting Impact on the Scientific Community

Samuel Park's contributions to the field of quantum mechanics and subatomic research have not only advanced scientific understanding but also transformed the culture of scientific inquiry itself. His unique approach combined rigorous scientific methodology with an unconventional use of humor, making complex theories more accessible and engaging to both the scientific community and the public at large.

Redefining Scientific Communication

One of Samuel's most significant impacts was his ability to bridge the gap between complex scientific concepts and public understanding. He recognized that the language of science could often be a barrier, alienating those outside the field. To address this, he developed a series of public lectures and workshops that integrated comedy into the presentation of scientific ideas. For example, during his talk on quantum entanglement, he famously quipped, "If you think your relationship is complicated, try being two particles that are light-years apart but still know what each other is thinking!" This approach not only entertained but also facilitated a deeper understanding of intricate theories.

Innovative Educational Programs

In addition to his public outreach, Samuel established innovative educational programs aimed at inspiring young scientists. The Park Foundation for Scientific Advancement created a curriculum that emphasized creativity alongside traditional scientific education. This program included hands-on experiments, collaborative projects, and, notably, comedy workshops that encouraged students to express scientific concepts through humor. The success of these programs is evident in the growing number of students pursuing careers in science, technology, engineering, and mathematics (STEM) fields who credit Samuel's influence in their decision-making.

Collaborative Research Initiatives

Samuel's impact extended into collaborative research initiatives that fostered interdisciplinary partnerships. He believed that the best scientific advancements often arise from the intersection of diverse fields. For instance, his collaboration with artists and musicians led to the creation of the "Quantum Symphony," a multimedia project that used sound and visual art to illustrate quantum phenomena. This innovative approach not only captivated audiences but also inspired new ways of thinking about scientific representation.

Mentorship and Leadership in the Scientific Community

As a mentor, Samuel dedicated himself to nurturing the next generation of scientists. His open-door policy and approachable demeanor encouraged young researchers to seek guidance and share their ideas, fostering a culture of collaboration and support. Many of his mentees have gone on to make significant contributions to the field, often attributing their success to the encouragement and unconventional wisdom provided by Samuel. He often stated, "A great scientist is not just one who discovers; they are one who inspires others to discover."

Legacy of Humor in Science

The legacy of Samuel Park is also reflected in the growing acceptance of humor as a tool in scientific discourse. His influence has encouraged scientists to incorporate humor into their presentations and writings, making science more relatable and enjoyable. This shift has led to an increase in public engagement with science, as audiences are more likely to connect with and remember information that is presented in an entertaining manner.

Quantifying Impact: Metrics and Recognition

To quantify his impact, Samuel's work has been recognized through numerous awards and honors, including the prestigious Quantum Innovation Award. Metrics such as increased public attendance at science events, higher enrollment in STEM programs, and positive media coverage of scientific topics can be directly attributed to his efforts. For example, a study conducted by the National Science Foundation reported a 40% increase in public interest in quantum physics following Samuel's public lectures, demonstrating the effectiveness of his approach.

Conclusion: A Lasting Influence

In conclusion, Samuel Park's lasting impact on the scientific community is characterized by his innovative methods of communication, commitment to education, and dedication to mentorship. His legacy is not only evident in the advancements he made in quantum mechanics but also in the cultural shift he inspired within the scientific community. By embracing humor and creativity, Samuel Park has shown that science can be both profound and entertaining, leaving an indelible mark that will influence generations to come. As he often said, "Science is not just about answers; it's about the joy of asking the right questions—and maybe cracking a few jokes along the way."

Incorporating Comedy into Science Education

The integration of comedy into science education has emerged as an innovative approach to engage students and enhance their understanding of complex scientific concepts. Samuel Park, in his quest to demystify the subatomic world, recognized that humor could serve as a powerful tool to foster curiosity and facilitate learning. This section explores the theoretical underpinnings of using comedy in education, the challenges faced, and practical examples that illustrate its effectiveness.

Theoretical Foundations

The use of humor in education is supported by several psychological theories. One such theory is the **Incongruity Theory**, which posits that humor arises when there is a discrepancy between expectations and reality. This unexpected twist can lead to laughter, which not only entertains but also enhances memory retention. According to [1], humor can create a positive emotional climate, which is conducive to learning.

Additionally, the **Cognitive Load Theory** suggests that reducing cognitive overload can improve learning outcomes. By presenting complex information through humorous anecdotes or relatable scenarios, educators can simplify difficult concepts, making them more accessible. As noted by [2], humor can lower students' anxiety levels, allowing them to engage more fully with the material.

Challenges in Implementation

Despite its advantages, incorporating comedy into science education is not without challenges. One significant issue is the risk of trivializing serious scientific concepts. Educators must strike a balance between humor and the integrity of the subject matter. As emphasized by [3], if humor is perceived as a distraction rather than a tool for understanding, it can undermine the learning objectives.

Another challenge lies in the diverse backgrounds and sensitivities of students. What is humorous to one group may not resonate with another, potentially alienating some learners. Thus, it is crucial for educators to be mindful of their audience and to select humor that is inclusive and appropriate.

Practical Examples

Samuel Park's approach to incorporating comedy in science education can be illustrated through several practical examples:

- **Quantum Comedy Nights:** Samuel organized events where scientists presented their research using stand-up comedy. For instance, he might explain quantum superposition with a joke about Schrödinger's cat, highlighting the paradox with a humorous twist: "Why did Schrödinger's cat cross the road? Because it was both alive and dead on the other side!" This approach not only made the concept memorable but also encouraged students to explore quantum mechanics further.

- **Animated Educational Videos:** Samuel collaborated with animators to create short videos that combined scientific explanations with comedic narratives. For example, a video explaining the uncertainty principle might feature a character who is hilariously indecisive, embodying the essence of uncertainty in a relatable manner. The humor in the animation keeps students engaged while effectively conveying complex ideas.

- **Interactive Workshops:** In his workshops, Samuel employed role-playing games where students acted out scientific principles. For example, to explain the concept of entanglement, students could perform a skit where they are "entangled" in a humorous situation that requires them to communicate without directly interacting. This method not only reinforces the concept but also fosters teamwork and creativity.

Conclusion

Incorporating comedy into science education, as exemplified by Samuel Park, offers a dynamic way to engage students and enhance their understanding of complex concepts. While challenges exist, the benefits of humor in creating a positive learning environment and improving information retention are significant. By embracing humor as a catalyst for innovation, educators can inspire the next generation of scientists to dream big and explore the wonders of the universe with curiosity and joy.

Bibliography

[1] Ziv, A. (1988). *Teaching and Learning with Humor*. Journal of Educational Psychology, 80(2), 250-253.

[2] Meyer, J. (2000). *Humor in Education: A Review of the Literature*. Journal of Educational Psychology, 92(2), 258-267.

[3] Tindall-Ford, S., Chandler, P., & Sweller, J. (2006). *Cognitive Load Theory and the Use of Humor in Education*. Educational Psychology Review, 18(2), 155-172.

Conclusion

Samuel Park: Pioneer of Subatomic Discoveries

Reflections on a Life Devoted to Science

Samuel Park's journey through the intricate landscapes of quantum mechanics was not merely a professional pursuit; it was a profound exploration of existence itself. His reflections on a life devoted to science reveal a tapestry woven from curiosity, resilience, and an unwavering belief in the power of inquiry. This section delves into the philosophical underpinnings of his scientific endeavors, the challenges he faced, and the transformative impact of his work on both the scientific community and the broader public.

The Philosophical Underpinning of Scientific Inquiry

At the heart of Samuel's scientific philosophy lay a deep-seated belief in the interconnectedness of all things. Inspired by the principles of quantum entanglement, he often mused about the implications of this phenomenon not only for physics but for understanding the fabric of reality itself. Quantum entanglement, described mathematically by the equation:

$$|\psi\rangle = \sum_i c_i |a_i\rangle \otimes |b_i\rangle$$

illustrates how particles can become linked, such that the state of one instantly influences the state of another, regardless of the distance separating them. Samuel saw this as a metaphor for human relationships, emphasizing the idea that our actions resonate far beyond our immediate surroundings.

Challenges and Resilience

Despite his groundbreaking achievements, Samuel's path was littered with obstacles. The scientific community, often resistant to unconventional ideas, posed significant challenges. Critics dismissed his radical theories, labeling them as whimsical rather than scientifically valid. Samuel faced moments of self-doubt, particularly during the development of his Quantum Microscope, which he envisioned as a tool to unveil the hidden beauty of the subatomic world.

He often recalled a pivotal moment when he presented his ideas at a prestigious conference. The audience, filled with established scientists, reacted with skepticism. Yet, Samuel's resilience shone through. He responded to the criticism not with defensiveness but with humor, quipping, "If I had a quantum particle for every time someone doubted me, I'd have enough to power a small city!" This ability to blend comedy with serious scientific discourse not only disarmed his critics but also endeared him to many, illustrating the importance of humor in navigating the often-stressful world of scientific inquiry.

The Transformative Power of Discovery

As Samuel reflected on his life, he recognized that the essence of scientific pursuit lies in the joy of discovery. His first major breakthrough, the Quantum Microscope, was not just a technological advancement; it was a gateway to a new realm of understanding. The ability to visualize particles at a subatomic level allowed scientists to explore phenomena previously thought to be beyond reach. Samuel's work exemplified the principle articulated by physicist Richard Feynman, who famously stated, "The imagination of nature is far greater than the imagination of man."

With the Quantum Microscope, Samuel unveiled the intricate dance of electrons and protons, providing visual representations that captivated both scientists and the public alike. This democratization of science—making complex concepts accessible—was a cornerstone of his legacy. He often said, "Science should be like a good joke; it should resonate, provoke thought, and above all, be understood."

Legacy and Inspiration

Samuel's reflections also encompassed his desire to inspire future generations. He established the Park Foundation for Scientific Advancement, aimed at nurturing young minds and fostering curiosity. His mentoring style was characterized by an emphasis on creativity and humor. He believed that the next generation of scientists should not only be equipped with knowledge but also encouraged to explore the world with a sense of wonder and playfulness.

In his workshops, Samuel would often employ comedic techniques to explain complex scientific concepts. For example, he famously used the analogy of a "quantum magician" to describe the principles of superposition, illustrating how particles could exist in multiple states simultaneously until observed. This approach not only made learning enjoyable but also helped demystify intricate theories for students of all ages.

Embracing Humor as a Catalyst for Innovation

Ultimately, Samuel Park's life and work exemplified the profound connection between humor and innovation. He understood that laughter has the power to break down barriers, foster collaboration, and ignite creativity. As he often remarked, "Science without humor is like a joke without a punchline; it misses the point."

His reflections on the role of humor in science extended beyond his personal experiences. Samuel advocated for a culture where humor is embraced in academic settings, arguing that it could lead to more open-minded discussions and innovative thinking. He encouraged scientists to share their failures and frustrations with a lighthearted perspective, promoting an environment where experimentation and risk-taking were celebrated rather than feared.

Conclusion

In closing, Samuel Park's reflections on a life devoted to science reveal a multifaceted individual whose journey was marked by curiosity, resilience, and a commitment to inspiring others. His belief in the interconnectedness of all things, the transformative power of discovery, and the importance of humor in scientific discourse left an indelible mark on the scientific community. As we ponder his legacy, we are reminded that the pursuit of knowledge is not merely a solitary endeavor but a shared journey, one that thrives on collaboration, creativity, and above all, the joy of discovery.

> "Science is not only about finding answers; it's about asking the right questions, embracing the unknown, and laughing along the way."

The Legacy of Quantum Dreams

The legacy of Samuel Park's work in the realm of quantum mechanics extends far beyond his personal achievements and accolades. His groundbreaking discoveries and innovative approaches have set a new standard in scientific inquiry, inspiring a generation of researchers and dreamers to explore the mysteries of the universe. The essence of his legacy can be encapsulated in four key themes: the democratization of science, the integration of humor in education, the nurturing of curiosity, and the advancement of technology.

Democratization of Science

Samuel Park believed that science should not be an exclusive domain reserved for a select few. He championed the idea that scientific knowledge and inquiry should be accessible to everyone, regardless of their background. This philosophy was evident in his establishment of the Park Foundation for Scientific Advancement, which aimed to provide resources, mentorship, and funding to aspiring scientists from underrepresented communities.

By hosting workshops, lectures, and public demonstrations, Samuel encouraged individuals to engage with scientific concepts that were often deemed too complex or esoteric. His efforts resulted in a significant increase in public interest in quantum mechanics and the sciences, as evidenced by the rise in enrollment in STEM (Science, Technology, Engineering, and Mathematics) programs across various educational institutions.

Integration of Humor in Education

One of the most distinctive aspects of Samuel Park's legacy is his unique approach to science communication. Drawing inspiration from the comedic style of Steve Martin, he employed humor as a tool to demystify complex scientific theories. By using wit and levity, he made quantum mechanics not only approachable but also enjoyable for the general public.

For instance, during his lectures, Samuel would often use humorous analogies to explain intricate concepts such as quantum entanglement. He likened entangled particles to a pair of socks in a dryer—once they are entangled, no matter how far apart they are, if one sock is lost, the other will always be affected. This playful approach to teaching encouraged students to embrace their curiosity without the fear of failure or misunderstanding.

Nurturing Curiosity

Samuel Park's legacy is also characterized by his unwavering commitment to nurturing curiosity in others. He firmly believed that curiosity is the driving force behind innovation and scientific discovery. Throughout his career, he mentored countless students and young scientists, instilling in them the importance of asking questions and seeking answers.

In his mentorship programs, Samuel emphasized the significance of experimental learning. He encouraged his mentees to design their own experiments, even if they seemed unconventional or impractical. This hands-on approach led to the development of numerous projects that challenged existing scientific paradigms and resulted in new insights into quantum phenomena.

Advancement of Technology

The technological advancements stemming from Samuel Park's research have had a profound impact on various fields, including communications, computing, and materials science. His invention of the quantum microscope revolutionized the way scientists visualize and understand the subatomic world.

The quantum microscope, based on the principles of quantum superposition and entanglement, allows researchers to observe particles at unprecedented resolutions. The mathematical foundation for this technology is rooted in the wave-particle duality described by the de Broglie hypothesis:

$$\lambda = \frac{h}{p} \qquad (40)$$

where λ is the wavelength associated with a particle, h is Planck's constant, and p is the momentum of the particle. This equation underscores the dual nature of particles, which is central to quantum mechanics and serves as a basis for the quantum microscope's functionality.

Furthermore, Samuel's work on quantum entanglement has led to the development of quantum communication technologies, including quantum key distribution (QKD). QKD enables secure communication channels by utilizing the principles of entanglement to detect eavesdropping attempts. The security of QKD can be mathematically represented by the following inequality, known as the Bell inequality:

$$S = |E(a,b) + E(a,b') + E(a',b) - E(a',b')| \leq 2 \qquad (41)$$

where S is the Bell parameter, and $E(a,b)$ represents the correlation between measurements on entangled particles. This inequality highlights the non-classical correlations that arise from entangled states, further validating the implications of Samuel's discoveries.

Conclusion

In conclusion, the legacy of Samuel Park is a multifaceted tapestry woven from threads of curiosity, humor, accessibility, and technological advancement. His contributions to quantum mechanics and his innovative teaching methods have left an indelible mark on the scientific community and society at large. As future innovators continue to build upon his work, they do so with the knowledge that the pursuit of knowledge is not only a serious endeavor but also an opportunity for joy, creativity, and connection. Samuel Park's journey exemplifies the idea that through dreaming big and embracing humor, we can push the boundaries of what is possible in science and beyond.

Inspiring the World to Dream Big and Push Boundaries

Samuel Park's journey through the intricate landscape of quantum mechanics serves as a beacon for aspiring scientists and innovators around the globe. His life encapsulates the essence of dreaming big and pushing the boundaries of what is deemed possible. This section explores how Samuel's philosophy, coupled with his groundbreaking discoveries, inspires others to transcend limitations and embrace the unknown.

The Power of Vision

At the core of Samuel's success was his unwavering vision—an ability to see beyond the present realities of science. Visionary thinking is often rooted in the capacity to imagine future possibilities that do not yet exist. Samuel's early fascination with the subatomic world was not merely an academic pursuit; it was a profound commitment to uncovering the mysteries of existence.

$$E = mc^2 \qquad (42)$$

This foundational equation, formulated by Albert Einstein, illustrates the equivalence of mass and energy, underpinning much of modern physics. Samuel took this concept further, envisioning applications that could revolutionize technology and communication. His relentless pursuit of knowledge and understanding led him to explore quantum entanglement, a phenomenon that would later redefine the boundaries of communication.

Overcoming Challenges

Samuel's journey was not without its hurdles. The scientific community is often resistant to unconventional ideas, and Samuel faced skepticism and criticism at every turn. However, these challenges only fueled his determination. He embraced the notion that failure is a stepping stone to success.

$$F = ma \tag{43}$$

In this equation, F represents force, m is mass, and a is acceleration. Samuel applied this principle to his life, understanding that the force of his passion and intellect could overcome the mass of doubt and inertia within the scientific community. His ability to accelerate his research through persistence and creativity exemplifies how challenges can be transformed into opportunities for growth.

Innovative Thinking and Humor

One of the most remarkable aspects of Samuel's approach was his incorporation of humor into the scientific discourse. He believed that laughter could break down barriers and make complex concepts more accessible. By using comedic elements in his presentations, he not only engaged audiences but also encouraged a culture of curiosity and creativity.

$$\text{Humor} = \text{Surprise} + \text{Incongruity} \tag{44}$$

This equation highlights the fundamental components of humor, which Samuel skillfully integrated into his lectures and research discussions. By presenting scientific ideas in a light-hearted manner, he inspired others to view science as an exciting adventure rather than a daunting challenge. This approach not only made his work more relatable but also encouraged others to explore their own innovative ideas without fear of judgment.

Mentorship and Legacy

Samuel understood that inspiring the next generation required more than just personal achievements; it necessitated a commitment to mentorship. Through the establishment of the Park Foundation for Scientific Advancement, he created a platform for aspiring scientists to explore their passions, experiment with radical ideas, and embrace failure as a part of the learning process.

$$\text{Inspiration} = \text{Education} + \text{Empowerment} \quad (45)$$

This equation encapsulates Samuel's philosophy of mentorship. By providing education and empowerment, he instilled confidence in young innovators, encouraging them to dream big and pursue their own groundbreaking discoveries. His legacy is not only defined by his scientific contributions but also by the countless individuals he inspired to push boundaries.

Conclusion

In conclusion, Samuel Park's life serves as a testament to the power of dreaming big and pushing boundaries. His visionary thinking, ability to overcome challenges, innovative use of humor, and commitment to mentorship have left an indelible mark on the scientific community. As we reflect on his journey, we are reminded that the pursuit of knowledge is not merely about the discoveries we make but also about the inspiration we ignite in others.

Through his story, we learn that the future of innovation lies in our willingness to dream beyond the horizon, challenge the status quo, and embrace the journey of exploration—where every question leads to new possibilities and every setback becomes a catalyst for greater achievements.

Embracing Humor as a Catalyst for Innovation

Humor has long been recognized as a powerful tool in various fields, from education to corporate environments. In the realm of scientific innovation, humor serves as a catalyst that fosters creativity, encourages collaboration, and enhances communication. Samuel Park, with his unique blend of scientific rigor and comedic flair, exemplifies how humor can be harnessed to break down barriers and inspire groundbreaking discoveries.

Theoretical Foundations of Humor in Innovation

The integration of humor into the innovation process can be understood through several psychological and sociological theories. One of the most relevant theories is the *Incongruity Theory*, which posits that humor arises when there is a discrepancy between what is expected and what actually occurs. This incongruity can stimulate cognitive flexibility, allowing individuals to approach problems from new angles. In the context of scientific research, this flexibility is crucial for innovative thinking.

Moreover, the *Benign Violation Theory* suggests that humor can arise from situations that are simultaneously perceived as a violation of social norms and benign. In scientific discourse, this can translate to challenging established norms or questioning accepted theories in a light-hearted manner, thus promoting a culture of open inquiry and experimentation.

The Role of Humor in Problem-Solving

Humor not only enhances creativity but also plays a vital role in problem-solving. When individuals are in a positive emotional state, often induced by humor, they are more likely to engage in divergent thinking—an essential component of creative problem-solving. Research has shown that laughter can increase the levels of dopamine in the brain, leading to enhanced cognitive function and improved memory retention.

For instance, Samuel Park often used humor in his presentations and lectures to simplify complex concepts. By incorporating jokes and anecdotes, he made quantum mechanics more accessible to audiences who might otherwise feel intimidated by the subject matter. This approach not only engaged his listeners but also encouraged them to think critically about the material.

Examples of Humor in Scientific Innovation

Several notable examples illustrate how humor has been successfully integrated into scientific innovation:

- **Richard Feynman**, a renowned physicist, was famous for his playful approach to science. He often used humor in his lectures to captivate students and make physics more relatable. His ability to convey complex ideas with levity inspired a generation of scientists and thinkers.

- **Carl Sagan**, the beloved astronomer and science communicator, frequently employed humor in his writing and public speaking. His witty remarks and engaging storytelling made astrophysics accessible to the general public, igniting a passion for science in many.

- In contemporary science communication, platforms like **YouTube** have seen the rise of channels such as *MinutePhysics* and *SciShow*, where creators use humor to explain scientific concepts. These channels have garnered millions of views, demonstrating that humor can effectively engage and educate diverse audiences.

Challenges and Misconceptions

Despite the clear benefits of incorporating humor into scientific discourse, there are challenges and misconceptions that must be addressed. One common misconception is that humor undermines the seriousness of scientific inquiry. On the contrary, humor can coexist with rigorous scientific standards; it can enhance the communication of complex ideas without diluting their importance.

Another challenge is the potential for humor to alienate certain audiences. Humor is often subjective, and what resonates with one group may not with another. Therefore, it is essential for innovators like Samuel Park to be mindful of their audience and tailor their comedic approach accordingly.

Conclusion: The Legacy of Humor in Science

Samuel Park's legacy as a pioneer of subatomic discoveries is inextricably linked to his embrace of humor as a catalyst for innovation. By integrating comedy into his scientific practice, he not only made complex concepts more approachable but also fostered an environment of creativity and collaboration. His approach serves as a model for future innovators, emphasizing the importance of humor in breaking down barriers and inspiring the next generation of thinkers.

In conclusion, embracing humor in scientific innovation is not merely a whimsical choice; it is a strategic approach that can lead to profound insights and breakthroughs. As we continue to explore the mysteries of the universe, let us remember the power of laughter as a vital ingredient in the recipe for innovation.

Index

-doubt, 4, 8, 80

a, 1–21, 25–33, 35–43, 46–50, 52, 54, 58, 59, 61–75, 79–86, 88
ability, 2, 5, 7, 9, 11, 20, 35, 36, 38, 39, 46, 52, 61, 64, 66, 72
abstraction, 41
absurdity, 20, 27
abundance, 30
academic, 2, 3, 8, 10, 11, 16, 62, 81
acceptance, 69, 73
accessibility, 84
accuracy, 53
achievement, 62
act, 16, 27
action, 16
actor, 20
addition, 7, 20
adherence, 8
advancement, 9, 39, 82, 84
advantage, 61
advent, 61
adventure, 85
adversity, 18, 50
age, 1, 4, 5, 15, 17
air, 13, 45, 50
airport, 1

Albert Einstein, 6, 84
algorithm, 61
Alice, 64
alienation, 2
allure, 10
amusement, 43
analog, 26
analogy, 12
analysis, 25, 29
anecdote, 20, 49
announcement, 47, 50, 52
anxiety, 50, 71
apparatus, 9
appeal, 40, 46
application, 60, 62, 64
appreciation, 20, 40, 41, 68
approach, 4, 5, 7, 9, 11, 14, 18–21, 25–27, 33, 35, 36, 41, 43, 46, 47, 49, 52, 65–69, 72–75, 82, 83, 85, 87, 88
arrangement, 38
array, 30
arsenal, 32
art, 7, 18, 25, 26, 29, 40, 72
artist, 40
artistry, 41
atmosphere, 19, 21
atom, 7, 11, 40

attempt, 63
attention, 26, 29, 43, 45, 49, 53, 68
attitude, 18
audience, 12, 14, 20, 28, 36, 43, 46, 49, 51, 53, 54, 65, 66, 74, 88
audio, 19
auditorium, 50
award, 52
awareness, 65

background, 36, 69, 82
backyard, 1, 5
bag, 1
baking, 5
balance, 20, 53, 59
ball, 26
ballet, 40
barrage, 27
barrier, 4, 50, 72
basement, 29
battlefield, 47
beacon, 52
beam, 36
beauty, 4, 31, 39–41, 80
beginning, 7
behavior, 2, 3, 5, 7, 10, 29–31, 40
belief, 1, 5, 8, 17, 18, 21, 27, 29, 64, 69, 79, 81
benefit, 61
biology, 1, 4, 39
birthday, 31
birthplace, 29
blend, 5, 7, 20, 29, 31, 37, 86
Bob, 64
Bohr, 11
box, 16, 17, 27, 36, 53
branch, 10, 15
breakthrough, 12, 37

bridge, 17, 21, 40, 43, 64, 72
brilliance, 27
brink, 12, 62
building, 3, 7, 70
bulb, 6
buzz, 45

calibration, 9
camaraderie, 9
candidacy, 45, 47
capability, 38
capacity, 11, 41
carbon, 36
cardboard, 30
career, 7, 18, 29, 31, 37, 64, 83
case, 69
cat, 16, 49, 53, 65
catalyst, 13, 15, 18, 75, 86, 88
center, 47
challenge, 12, 15, 27, 29, 32, 37, 58, 63–65, 74, 85, 88
chance, 13, 15
character, 9, 11
charm, 49
chemistry, 71
child, 3, 4, 11
childhood, 1, 3, 5, 10
choice, 88
circuit, 6
clarity, 11, 28, 38, 39, 45
classroom, 7, 8
climate, 12
closing, 81
club, 7
coat, 66
code, 63
coherence, 15
collaboration, 18, 21, 26, 49, 50, 64, 67–69, 72, 81, 86, 88

Index 91

colleague, 20
combination, 10, 19, 30, 31
comedian, 20
comedy, 5, 8, 12, 26, 31–33, 42, 52, 54, 65, 66, 72, 74, 75, 88
commitment, 17, 81, 83, 85
communication, 11, 16, 20, 33, 41, 43, 46, 51, 59, 61–64, 66, 68, 82, 84–86, 88
community, 8, 10, 25, 27, 29, 33, 41, 45, 47, 49, 50, 66, 68–70, 72, 79–81, 84
competition, 47, 49, 50
complexity, 41
comprehension, 26
computation, 61, 63
computer, 36
computing, 12, 15, 16, 46, 51, 58, 61, 62, 68, 83
concept, 3, 6, 11, 12, 16, 21, 26, 27, 53, 64, 65, 84
conclusion, 3, 10, 31, 36, 39, 47, 50, 59, 62, 66, 69, 84, 88
conference, 21, 49, 53
confidence, 4
confidentiality, 45
confluence, 35
connection, 84
consciousness, 27
constant, 69
content, 32, 52
context, 65
contrary, 88
contrast, 48
conversation, 47
core, 15, 17, 25
correction, 61, 63
cost, 71
counter, 30

courage, 29
coverage, 49
creation, 63, 72
creativity, 7, 12, 17, 18, 20, 21, 25–27, 29–32, 36, 41, 43, 47, 52, 64, 67–69, 80, 81, 84–86, 88
credibility, 48–50
criticism, 14, 26, 27, 29, 42
crucible, 31
cry, 29
cryptography, 51, 58, 61
culmination, 50
culture, 68, 69, 72, 81, 85
curiosity, 1–5, 7, 10, 12, 13, 15, 17, 19, 25, 27, 30, 33, 35, 41, 43, 52, 59, 66, 67, 69, 70, 74, 75, 79–85

danger, 32
day, 5, 13, 50
deadline, 46
decoherence, 61, 63
delivery, 26
democratization, 82
demonstration, 1, 26, 49
density, 40
departure, 18
design, 18, 36, 39, 83
designer, 7
desire, 16, 80
detail, 9, 15, 38
detection, 21, 37
detector, 30
determination, 7, 9, 16–18, 26, 59
development, 26, 45, 80, 83
device, 26, 35–37, 54
difficulty, 61
diffraction, 37

dinner, 4
discipline, 1
discourse, 21, 31, 42, 47, 53, 67, 69, 73, 81, 85, 88
discovery, 1, 11, 12, 25, 27, 41, 59, 69, 81, 83
discussion, 20, 47, 54, 70
disparity, 48
distance, 12, 16, 26, 37, 41, 59, 79
domain, 15, 39, 82
dose, 29
doubt, 4, 8, 29, 80
drama, 7
dream, 3, 10–12, 52, 75
drug, 12
duality, 5, 6, 10, 15, 30, 35, 39, 83
duration, 38

ecosystem, 67
edge, 27
education, 5, 7, 11, 31, 67, 71, 74, 75, 82, 86
effect, 27
effectiveness, 38, 74
efficiency, 71
Einstein, 16
electromagnetism, 6
electron, 7, 36, 40
elegance, 41
elitism, 49
Elizabeth Reynolds, 13, 15, 18, 29
Elizabeth Reynolds', 15
embrace, 3, 7, 9, 10, 12, 19, 27, 37, 43, 47, 59, 86, 88
emphasis, 5, 41, 68, 80
encounter, 13, 15
encouragement, 4, 5, 9, 14, 15
encryption, 46, 61
end, 1

endeavor, 10, 25, 31, 81, 84
energy, 4, 6, 10–12, 42, 84
engagement, 50, 54, 69, 73
engineering, 36
entanglement, 3, 8, 10, 12, 16, 18, 20, 25, 26, 29, 37, 41, 46, 53, 54, 58–64, 68, 70, 72, 79, 83, 85
entertainer, 20
entertainment, 31
enthusiasm, 3, 66
environment, 1, 3, 4, 14, 18, 20, 30, 32, 75, 81, 88
equation, 3, 4, 6, 8, 12, 29, 36, 40, 42, 46, 48, 70, 71, 79, 84, 85
equipment, 8, 18, 30
equivalence, 84
era, 64
eraser, 70
error, 61, 63
essence, 21, 29, 54, 82
establishment, 26, 68, 69, 82, 85
event, 21
evidence, 25
example, 2, 10, 12, 19, 20, 26, 30, 41, 54, 58, 63, 65, 68, 70, 72
excitement, 45, 47, 50
exhibit, 11, 15, 26, 35
existence, 40, 79
experience, 2, 6, 7, 9, 54
experiment, 5–7, 11, 16, 18, 26, 27, 29, 30, 36, 49, 70, 86
experimentation, 1, 8, 10, 25, 36, 59, 69, 81
explanation, 66
exploration, 1, 17, 31, 41, 59, 62, 79
explosion, 9
exposure, 10, 38

Index

expression, 31

fabric, 32, 62, 79
face, 5, 18, 26, 29, 49, 50
factor, 61
failure, 9, 18, 86
fair, 2, 13
familiarity, 53
family, 1–5, 29
fascination, 2, 3, 5, 6, 10, 15–17
father, 1
fear, 3, 85
feasibility, 36
feedback, 36
feeling, 20
fever, 46
Feynman, 11
fiction, 41–43
field, 6, 10, 14–16, 21, 31, 39, 45–47, 64, 72
figure, 49
Finch, 28
finding, 3
flair, 31, 86
flame, 4
force, 17, 83
form, 19, 20
formalism, 58
formulation, 11
foster, 74
foundation, 1, 5, 7, 10, 11, 27, 67–69, 83
fraction, 12
framework, 11, 58, 61
frenzy, 47
fridge, 54
frontier, 59
frustration, 18
function, 16, 40

functionality, 37
funding, 8, 49, 69, 82
fundraising, 69
fusion, 42
future, 1–3, 5, 7, 9, 10, 12, 15, 27, 29, 31, 33, 39, 43, 45, 46, 52, 59, 62, 66, 69, 80, 84, 88

game, 41
gap, 36, 40, 43, 66, 72
gaze, 13
Geiger, 30
generation, 12, 27, 38, 41, 47, 52, 64, 67–69, 75, 80, 82, 85, 88
genius, 35, 36
glass, 9
goal, 9
graduate, 8
graphene, 36, 38
ground, 5
groundbreaking, 3, 6, 9, 11, 15, 17, 18, 29, 37–39, 41, 45–47, 49, 59, 60, 64, 67, 80, 82, 86
groundwork, 5, 17, 31, 59, 63
group, 31, 65, 74, 88
growth, 5, 9, 10
guidance, 15

hallmark, 5, 19, 31, 36, 41
hand, 8, 30
health, 8
heart, 37, 40, 69, 79
heartedness, 36
Heisenberg, 40
Hilbert, 63
home, 1, 4, 29
hope, 50, 52

household, 1, 5, 8, 30
humor, 1, 5, 7, 8, 10–12, 14, 15, 17,
    19–21, 25–27, 29, 31–33,
    36, 37, 41–43, 46, 47, 49,
    50, 52–54, 64–69, 71–75,
    80–82, 84–88
hurdle, 63
hypothesis, 1, 8, 29, 83

idea, 3, 11, 15, 27, 79, 82, 84
image, 36, 48
imagination, 4, 11, 17
imaging, 35, 36, 38
impact, 35, 38, 39, 45, 46, 66, 68,
    72, 79, 83
implementation, 61
importance, 7, 9, 14, 17, 36, 49, 50,
    53, 64, 67, 71, 81, 83, 88
improvement, 46
incident, 9
incorporation, 21, 54, 85
increase, 73
individual, 36, 53, 58, 81
inequality, 58
influence, 5, 16, 73
information, 16, 38, 41, 58–61, 63,
    64, 73, 75
infrastructure, 61
ingenuity, 28, 30
ingredient, 88
innovation, 2, 7–9, 13, 15, 17, 18,
    27, 29, 31, 32, 35–37, 39,
    45, 47, 50, 52, 64, 67, 69,
    75, 83, 86–88
innovator, 7
inquiry, 4, 17, 20, 31, 35, 46, 47, 69,
    70, 72, 79, 82, 88
inquisitiveness, 1
insight, 35

inspiration, 11, 17, 36, 43, 49, 82
instability, 8
instance, 1, 7, 12, 18–21, 25, 27, 30,
    31, 38, 40, 42, 43, 49, 63,
    70, 72, 87
instrument, 36
integration, 33, 64, 67, 69, 74, 82
integrity, 32
intellect, 17, 20
intensity, 38
interconnectedness, 2, 79, 81
interdependence, 2
interest, 2, 5, 6, 10, 49
interference, 16, 30, 37–39
interplay, 47
intersection, 52, 72
interweave, 40
intrigue, 45
introduction, 37
intuition, 10, 15, 26, 59
invasion, 61
invention, 35–37, 39, 83
isolation, 9
issue, 38, 53

joke, 1, 3, 19, 65
journey, 3, 5, 7, 9, 10, 12, 15, 17, 20,
    25, 27, 29, 36, 41, 43, 47,
    50, 59, 62, 64, 66, 79, 81,
    84
joy, 12, 33, 66, 75, 81, 84
judge, 2
judgment, 85

key, 2, 37, 38, 58, 63, 67, 69, 82
kitchen, 5, 26
knowledge, 1, 3, 5, 7, 10, 17, 31, 36,
    37, 59, 67, 69, 71, 81, 82,
    84

Index 95

lab, 66
laboratory, 8, 9, 26, 29–31, 48
lack, 30
landscape, 3, 29, 41, 47, 50, 69
language, 4, 72
laser, 9, 30
lattice, 36, 38
laughter, 5, 7, 19, 21, 43, 54, 66, 71, 85, 88
layman, 49
lead, 3, 7, 15, 30, 38, 53, 81, 88
learning, 1, 9, 14, 18, 71, 74, 75, 83, 86
lecture, 20, 54
leftover, 54
legacy, 27, 41, 43, 64, 66, 69, 73, 81–84, 88
lens, 40, 41
level, 2, 4, 28, 30, 35, 38, 39, 59
levity, 7, 82
library, 3
life, 1, 5, 8, 10, 12, 20, 67, 79, 81
light, 1, 2, 5, 6, 10–12, 19, 21, 35, 36, 38, 39, 49, 72, 85
like, 5–7, 9, 11, 15, 18, 26, 35, 49, 67, 88
likelihood, 46
limit, 37
literacy, 64, 66, 69
literature, 17
location, 58, 60, 64
loneliness, 9

magnetism, 39
makeshift, 8, 29, 31, 48
making, 5, 12, 14, 15, 19, 32, 36, 41, 49, 51, 61, 63, 72, 73
male, 14
malfunction, 9

manner, 7, 21, 52, 64, 70, 73, 85
mark, 81, 84
Martin, 20, 21
marvel, 36
mass, 84
master, 10
material, 19, 21, 36, 53, 66, 87
mathematician, 19
matter, 10, 19, 20, 25, 43, 53, 87
maverick, 48
Max Planck, 17
Maya Chen, 68
mean, 16
means, 26
measurement, 16, 38
mechanism, 5, 8, 27, 36
media, 46, 47, 49
meeting, 18
mentor, 13
mentorship, 7, 13–15, 67, 82, 83, 85
merit, 52
message, 53, 66
metaphor, 79
method, 1, 14, 20, 43, 52, 63, 68
methodology, 72
microscope, 9, 15, 36, 54, 83
microscopy, 37–39, 45
milestone, 69
mind, 1, 16, 69
mindset, 17
misconception, 88
misdirection, 20
mission, 67, 69
misunderstanding, 20, 65
misuse, 61
mix, 28, 30
mixture, 50
model, 7, 11, 88
modeling, 12

moment, 1, 13, 29, 36, 47, 62
momentum, 40
mood, 5
mother, 1, 4
motion, 15
multimedia, 72
museum, 1

nanotechnology, 38, 39
narrative, 20, 66
nature, 2, 3, 7, 10, 12, 20, 41, 47, 49
necessity, 67
need, 50, 64, 67
network, 9, 63, 69
niche, 47
Niels Bohr, 6, 11, 17
night, 9
noise, 38, 39, 61, 63
nomination, 45, 46
non, 8, 67
none, 13
norm, 15
notion, 17, 26
nurturing, 4, 67, 69, 80, 82, 83

objection, 28
observation, 1, 16, 27, 46
observer, 16, 27
obstacle, 10
odyssey, 47
Ohm, 6
one, 2, 3, 5, 8, 16, 19–21, 26, 50, 58–60, 64, 66, 68, 70, 71, 74, 79, 81, 88
opening, 39, 54
openness, 69
operation, 64
opportunity, 69, 84
organization, 67

originality, 45
other, 12, 13, 16, 26, 49, 72
outlet, 9
outlook, 18
outreach, 67
outset, 8
oversight, 9
oversimplification, 32

pair, 12, 58
panel, 54
paradigm, 46
parallel, 20
Park, 39
part, 9, 10, 29, 86
particle, 5, 6, 10, 11, 15, 16, 20, 21, 30, 35, 39, 59, 60, 64, 83
party, 31
passion, 3, 6, 9, 13, 15, 18, 41, 69
path, 2, 4, 7, 8, 10, 11, 18, 20, 80
pattern, 16
peer, 27
pendulum, 6
perception, 11, 29, 39, 47, 49
performance, 26
period, 3, 6, 8
perseverance, 2, 31, 64
perspective, 3, 17, 19, 31, 35, 81
phase, 1, 39
phenomenon, 3, 16, 21, 35, 37, 38, 40, 59, 62, 64, 79, 85
philosophy, 14, 26, 79, 82
photobleaching, 38, 39
photon, 1, 42
photosynthesis, 4
physicist, 13, 15, 18, 19
physics, 1–3, 5, 6, 10, 12, 15, 17, 39, 58, 66, 71, 79, 84
piece, 30

Index

pioneer, 9, 10, 15, 27, 88
pitch, 46
pizza, 54
place, 13, 26
placement, 6
plant, 4
platform, 86
playfulness, 81
playground, 7, 26
point, 2, 71
pointer, 30
position, 40
potential, 5, 11, 16, 29, 38, 39, 45–47, 51, 61–65, 88
power, 6, 12, 15, 27, 50, 61, 79, 81, 88
practice, 64, 88
precision, 39
present, 2, 21, 49
presentation, 13, 21, 28, 72
pressure, 8
principle, 6, 20, 25, 66
privacy, 61
probability, 11, 40
problem, 32, 42
process, 4, 9, 20, 38, 45, 58, 60, 61, 64, 86
professor, 1
program, 3
project, 2, 4, 6, 7, 13, 71, 72
promise, 64
proposal, 2
protein, 38
protocol, 58, 63
proton, 36
prototype, 9
prowess, 2, 20
public, 7, 17, 19, 36, 40, 41, 43, 47, 49, 50, 52, 64, 66, 72, 73, 79, 82
punchline, 20, 26
purification, 71
pursuit, 3, 5, 9–12, 17, 26, 31, 59, 79, 81, 84

quality, 12, 36, 38, 61
quantum, 1–21, 25–27, 29–31, 35–41, 43, 45–47, 49, 51, 53, 54, 58–64, 66–68, 70, 72, 79, 82–85, 87
qubit, 64
quest, 17, 62, 64, 74
question, 4, 14
questioning, 8, 69, 70
quo, 10, 27

radiation, 30
reach, 69
reality, 3, 12, 15, 16, 39, 59, 62, 79
realization, 9, 16
realm, 10, 15, 17, 20, 27, 31, 35, 38–41, 45–47, 59, 61, 82, 86
receiver, 60
reception, 53
recipe, 88
recognition, 45, 47, 49, 50
recovery, 63
reinterpretation, 27
relationship, 15, 53, 72
reliability, 63
reminder, 3, 12, 20, 29, 41, 66
representation, 7, 19, 38, 48, 64, 73
reputation, 9
research, 2, 3, 5, 9, 14, 18, 20, 26, 27, 29–33, 36, 38, 39, 45–47, 49, 63, 67, 72, 83, 85

resilience, 3–5, 9, 10, 12, 17, 26, 29, 50, 59, 79, 81
resistance, 17, 28
resolution, 35, 36, 39
resolve, 7, 10, 18, 36, 39
resourcefulness, 8
result, 64
retention, 26, 75
revolution, 62
Reynolds, 13–15
Richard Feynman, 11, 17
rigidity, 27
rigor, 25, 32, 46, 86
risk, 29, 32, 53, 81
role, 7, 11, 13, 25, 33, 46, 49, 58, 61, 66, 81
room, 50
rubber, 26
run, 9

s, 1–13, 15–21, 25–27, 29–31, 35–41, 43, 45–50, 52–54, 58, 59, 61–69, 71, 72, 75, 79–85, 88
sake, 9
sample, 36, 38
Samuel, 1–21, 25–32, 35–37, 39, 41–43, 45–50, 52–54, 58, 59, 63–67, 69–72, 79–81, 83–85
Samuel Park, 1, 5, 13, 17, 27, 29, 31, 33, 40, 41, 43, 50, 59, 62, 64, 67, 69, 73–75, 82, 84, 86–88
Samuel Park's, 3, 5, 7, 10, 12, 15, 17, 20, 25, 27, 29, 31, 35–39, 41, 45, 47, 50, 52, 61–64, 66, 69, 72, 75, 79, 81–84, 88

sanctuary, 31
scalability, 63
scale, 7, 39, 63
scenario, 11
scholarship, 68
school, 2–4, 6, 7
Schrödinger, 6, 16, 53
science, 1–7, 11–13, 15, 17, 18, 20, 25–27, 31–33, 36, 39, 41–43, 47, 52, 53, 61, 66–69, 71–75, 79, 81–85
scientist, 3, 10, 14, 26, 40, 48, 66
secrecy, 45
secret, 63
section, 20, 45, 47, 65, 74, 79
security, 46, 63
segue, 54
self, 4, 8, 80
sender, 60
sense, 1–4, 14, 41, 65, 81
series, 1, 3, 18, 21, 25, 26, 29, 36, 70, 72
seriousness, 5, 7, 42, 46, 88
session, 31, 54
set, 7, 9, 15, 17, 30, 82
setback, 2, 9
setting, 31, 47
setup, 30
shift, 3, 46, 73
Shor, 61
signal, 38
significance, 83
silence, 9
situation, 21
skepticism, 2, 8, 10, 14, 17, 18, 26, 27, 29, 36, 46, 48, 59, 69
skill, 2
slit, 5, 11, 16, 27, 30
society, 61, 84

Index 99

soda, 5
solitude, 9
sound, 19, 72
source, 17, 38, 43
space, 29–31, 50, 63
spark, 13, 26
speaking, 7, 49
specimen, 1
speculation, 45–47
spirit, 18, 26, 36, 37, 59, 69
sport, 18
spouse, 53
springboard, 43
stage, 7, 31, 47
standard, 82
state, 16, 27, 29, 38, 58, 59, 64, 79
statement, 67
status, 10, 27
Steve Martin, 82
Steve Martin's, 20, 49
Steve Martin, 20
stone, 9
story, 3, 20, 29, 50
storytelling, 7, 17, 20, 41, 43, 49
strategy, 49, 66
stress, 8
struggle, 69
study, 2, 39, 46
style, 17, 20, 41, 43, 49, 80, 82
subject, 19, 20, 43, 53, 68, 87
success, 50
summary, 5
summer, 3, 70
sunlight, 4
superconductivity, 39
superposition, 6, 11–13, 16, 21, 25, 37, 48, 49, 61, 83
support, 4, 5, 8, 9, 49
surface, 12

surrounding, 16, 45, 47, 50
surveillance, 61
swirling, 41
symbol, 8
system, 4, 7, 9, 16, 25, 71

t, 2, 18, 26
taking, 81
talent, 69
talk, 49, 72
tapestry, 40, 79, 84
task, 61
teacher, 1, 4, 6, 15
teaching, 5, 14, 84
team, 18, 20
technique, 20, 43, 66, 70
technology, 11, 29, 39, 59, 62, 82–84
teleportation, 58, 60, 64
tension, 50
test, 9, 29, 58
testament, 9, 50, 64
testing, 9
theme, 2
theorem, 58
theory, 8, 10, 14, 21, 25–27, 38, 58, 59, 64
thinker, 5
thinking, 17, 20, 26, 27, 72, 73, 81
Thompson, 6
thought, 8, 16, 37, 54
tightrope, 27
time, 3, 6, 7, 12, 36, 38, 61, 63
timeline, 9
timing, 26
today, 53
toll, 8
tool, 15, 19, 32, 65, 73, 74, 80, 82, 86
topic, 3, 6, 12
touch, 5, 27

town, 1
transfer, 6, 58–60, 64
transmission, 58, 60
treasure, 1
trip, 1
trove, 1
turn, 49
turning, 2, 31, 40
twist, 21, 43

uncertainty, 5, 6, 40, 66
underpinning, 84
understanding, 2, 4, 11, 14, 15, 17–19, 21, 25, 26, 30, 31, 36, 39–41, 43, 45, 59, 62, 64, 66, 69, 72, 74, 75, 79, 85
universe, 1, 3–5, 12, 17, 33, 39, 41, 43, 45, 59, 62, 66, 75, 82, 88
university, 3, 13
up, 5, 8, 19, 20, 36, 52, 54
upbringing, 5
use, 37, 61, 66, 72

validation, 9
validity, 29
variable, 58
variety, 5, 26
version, 70
video, 66
view, 17, 85
vinegar, 5
visibility, 49

vision, 12, 15, 49, 67
visit, 5
visualization, 35, 40
voice, 41, 49

wake, 67
water, 71
wave, 5, 6, 10, 11, 15, 16, 19, 30, 35, 39, 83
wavelength, 39
way, 1, 8, 11, 15, 29, 37, 52, 59, 75, 83
weight, 8
whole, 61
willingness, 4, 7, 10, 18, 37
wisdom, 12, 17, 25
wit, 49, 82
woman, 13
wonder, 1, 2, 14, 41, 81
work, 11, 13, 15, 18, 20, 21, 29, 36, 43, 45–47, 49–52, 63, 79, 82, 84, 85
workbench, 30
working, 18, 30
workshop, 70
workspace, 30
world, 1, 3, 5, 7, 10–13, 15–18, 25, 27, 31, 35, 37, 39–41, 43, 46, 47, 52, 54, 64, 70, 71, 74, 80, 81, 83
writer, 20

year, 3
yearning, 3